A Midsummer Night's Dream

William Shakespeare

THE EMC MASTERPIECE SERIES

Access Editions

SERIES EDITOR
Robert D. Shepherd

EMC/Paradigm Publishing
St. Paul, Minnesota

Staff Credits:
For **EMC/Paradigm Publishing**, St. Paul, Minnesota

Laurie Skiba
Editor

Eileen Slater
Editorial Consultant

Shannon O'Donnell Taylor
Associate Editor

Jennifer J. Anderson
Assistant Editor

For **Penobscot School Publishing, Inc.**, Danvers, Massachusetts

Editorial

Robert D. Shepherd
President, Executive Editor

Christina E. Kolb
Managing Editor

Sara Hyry
Editor

Laurie Faria
Associate Editor

Sharon Salinger
Copyeditor

Marilyn Murphy Shepherd
Editorial Advisor

Design and Production

Charles Q. Bent
Production Manager

Sara Day
Art Director

Diane Castro
Compositor

Janet Stebbings
Compositor

Published by EMC/Paradigm Publishing
875 Montreal Way
St. Paul, Minnesota 55102

Printed in the United States of America.
11 12 13 14 xxx 14 15 16 17

Table of Contents

William Shakespeare

William Shakespeare

William Shakespeare (1564–1616). William Shakespeare may well be the greatest dramatist the world has ever known. His mother, Mary Arden Shakespeare, was from a well-to-do, well-connected family. His father, John Shakespeare, was a prosperous glove maker and local politician. William's exact birthdate is unknown, but he was baptized in his hometown of Stratford-upon-Avon on April 26, 1564, and tradition has assigned him a birthdate of April 23, which was also the day of his death and the feast day of Saint George, England's patron saint.

Shakespeare attended the Stratford grammar school, where he studied Latin and perhaps some Greek. At the age of eighteen, Shakespeare married Anne Hathaway, eight years his senior, who was with child. Altogether, William and Anne had three children, a daughter Susanna and twins Hamnet and Judith. He may have worked for a while as a schoolteacher, for there are many references to teaching in his plays. By 1592, however, he was living in London and pursuing a life in the theater. Shakespeare continued to provide for his family and to expand his holdings in Stratford while living in London. He retired to Stratford-upon-Avon at the end of his life.

Shakespeare's Professional Career

By 1593, Shakespeare was a successful actor and playwright. His history plays *Henry the Sixth,* Parts 1, 2, and 3, and *The Tragedy of Richard the Third* had established him as a significant force in London theater. In 1593, when an outbreak of the plague forced the closing of the theaters, Shakespeare turned to narrative poetry, producing *Venus and Adonis* and *The Rape of Lucrece,* both dedicated to a patron, the Earl of Southampton. When the theaters reopened, Shakespeare plunged back into his primary vocation, and wrote thirty-seven plays in less than twenty years, including *The Taming of the Shrew; A Midsummer Night's Dream; The Merchant of Venice; Twelfth Night, or What You Will; All's Well That Ends Well; The Tragedy of King Richard the Second; The Tragedy of Romeo and Juliet; The Tragedy of Julius Cæsar; The Tragedy of Hamlet, Prince* of Denmark; *The Tragedy of Othello, the Moor of Venice; The Tragedy of King Lear; The Tragedy of Macbeth; The Winter's Tale;* and *The Tempest.*

Around 1594, Shakespeare became a shareholder in a theater company known as The Lord Chamberlain's Men. The troupe quickly became the most popular in London. By 1599, they were wealthy enough to build their own theater, a large open-air playhouse they called the Globe, and in 1603 they bought the Blackfriars, a small, artificially lighted indoor theater for winter performances. Their company began performing regularly at the court of Queen Elizabeth I. After the death of Elizabeth in 1603, Shakespeare's company became, officially, servants of King James I, and their name was changed to The King's Men. Shakespeare's final noncollaborative play, *The Famous History of the Life of Henry the Eighth,* was performed in London in 1613. Later that same year, he collaborated with John Fletcher to write a play called *The Two Noble Kinsmen.* At that time he was probably living again in Stratford, in a large house called New Place that he had bought in 1597. When he died in 1616, survived by his wife and his two daughters, Shakespeare was a wealthy man. He was buried in the Holy Trinity Church in Stratford-upon-Avon, where his bones rest to this day. The stone over his grave reads,

> Good frend for Jesus sake forbeare,
> To digg the dust encloased heare:
> Blest be the man that spares thes stones,
> And curst be he that moves my bones.

The Publication of Shakespeare's Plays

Shakespeare did not personally prepare his plays for publication, and no official collection of them appeared until after his death. A collection of his sonnets, considered by critics to be among the best poetry ever written in English, appeared in 1609. Many individual plays were published during his lifetime in unauthorized editions known as quartos. Many of these quartos are quite unreliable. Some were probably based on actors' memories of the plays. Some were reprintings of so-called prompter's copies used in production of the plays. Some may have been based on final manuscript versions produced by the author. In 1623, seven years after Shakespeare's death, his friends and fellow actors John Heminge and Henry Condell published a collected edition of thirty-five of Shakespeare's plays. This collection is known to literary historians as the First Folio. In the centuries since 1623, and especially during the last century and a half, editors have worked diligently to compare the various early printed versions of Shakespeare's works to determine which version or versions of each play best represent Shakespeare's intent.

Shakespeare's Finest Achievement

Fragments can be tantalizing. They tempt people, awakening a desire to reconstruct the missing pieces. Since very little is known of Shakespeare's life beyond a few official records and mentions by others in diaries or letters, many people have been driven to speculate about the private life of England's greatest author. Such speculation is made all the more difficult by the fact that Shakespeare did not write in a personal vein, about himself, but rather concentrated his vision on the lives of others. Reading his plays, or seeing them performed, we come to know many of his characters better than we know most people in our lives. A characteristic of Shakespeare's greatness is that his work takes us on journeys into parallel universes, into other minds, so that his characters' innermost feelings, dreams, wishes, values, motivations, and even contradictions become accessible. This is, perhaps, Shakespeare's finest achievement.

The Authorship of Shakespeare's Plays

The fact that Shakespeare was a commoner and led, according to the few facts we have, a rather ordinary life, has led many people to speculate that his plays were written by someone else—by the Earl of Oxford, perhaps, or by Ben Jonson, but there are good reasons to believe that Shakespeare was, indeed, the author of the plays attributed to him. One reason to accept the traditional attribution is that the plays show an understanding of the lives of people in all stations of life, from the lowliest peasants to men and women of the court. We know that Shakespeare came from a middle-class background and later moved in court circles, and this fact is consistent with his understanding of people from all walks of life. At the very least, a careful reader must conclude that the plays attributed to Shakespeare are the work of a single author, for they have a distinct voice not to be found in the work of any other dramatist of his day—a voice that has enriched our language as none other has ever done.

The Uniqueness of Shakespeare's Work

No brief summary can begin to catalog the many virtues of Shakespeare's work. He was a gifted observer of people, capable of creating unforgettable characters from all stations and walks of life. He used one of the largest vocabularies ever employed by an author, filling his plays with concrete details and with speech that, while not always realistic, is always engaging and believable. His plays probe the range of human experience. They are romantic in the sense that they are full of intensely conveyed passion. However, the plays rarely strain credibility or sink into sensationalism or sentimentality. Shakespeare's language tends to be dense, metaphorical, full of puns and word play, and yet natural, so that it comes "trippingly off the tongue" of an actor. A scene of Shakespeare tears across the stage, riveting and dramatic, and yet it bears close rereading, revealing in that rereading astonishing depth and complexity. Shakespeare wrote his dramas in a combination of prose, rhymed poetry, and blank verse always appropriate to the character or scene at hand. His plays have contributed many now well-known phrases to the English language. They have inspired audiences to laughter, joy, pity, fear, sadness, despair, and suspense for over four hundred years. In fact, his works have been performed more often and in more countries around the world than those of any other dramatist. To begin to read Shakespeare is to enter a world, one might say the world, for his art is, as Hamlet says it should be, "a mirror held up to nature"—to human nature. To read him well is to begin to understand others and ourselves. As Ben Jonson wrote, Shakespeare's art is "not of an age, but for all time."

Time Line of Shakespeare's Life

April 23, 1564	William Shakespeare is born in Stratford-upon-Avon, to parents Mary Arden Shakespeare and John Shakespeare.
April 26, 1564	William Shakespeare is baptized.
1582	William Shakespeare marries Anne Hathaway.
1583	Shakespeare's first daughter, Susanna, is born and christened.
1585	Anne Hathaway Shakespeare gives birth to twins: a boy, Hamnet, and a girl, Judith.
1589–1591	Shakespeare's first histories, *Henry the Sixth,* Parts 1 and 2, are produced.
1592–1593	*The Tragedy of Richard the Third* is produced. Not long afterward, the plague afflicts London and the theaters close. Shakespeare writes *Venus and Adonis* and *The Rape of Lucrece.*
1592–1594	Shakespeare's first comedy, *The Comedy of Errors,* is produced.
c. 1593	Shakespeare begins his sonnet cycle.
1593–1594	*The Taming of the Shrew* is produced.
1594–1595	*Love's Labor's Lost* is produced.
1595	*The Tragedy of King Richard the Second* is produced.
1595–1596	*The Tragedy of Romeo and Juliet* and *A Midsummer Night's Dream* are produced.
1596–1597	*The Merchant of Venice* and *Henry the Fourth,* Part 1, are produced.
1596	Shakespeare's son, Hamnet, dies at age eleven.
1597	Shakespeare acquires a fine home called New Place in Stratford-upon-Avon.
1597	Shakespeare produces *The Merry Wives of Windsor,* possibly at the request of Queen Elizabeth I.
1598	Shakespeare produces *Henry the Fourth,* Part 2.
1598–1599	*Much Ado about Nothing* is produced.
1599	*The Life of Henry the Fifth, The Tragedy of Julius Cæsar,* and *As You Like It* are produced.

Shakespeare's Globe Theater opens. | 1599

The Tragedy of Hamlet, Prince of Denmark is produced. | 1600–1601

Twelfth Night, or What You Will and *The History of Troilus and Cressida* are produced. | 1601–1602

All's Well That Ends Well is produced. | 1602–1603

Queen Elizabeth I dies. Shakespeare's troupe serves James I and becomes known as the King's Men. | 1603

Measure for Measure and *The Tragedy of Othello, the Moor of Venice* are produced. | 1604

The Tragedy of King Lear is produced. | 1605

The Tragedy of Macbeth is produced. | 1606

The Tragedy of Antony and Cleopatra is produced. | 1607

The Tragedy of Coriolanus and *Pericles, Prince of Tyre* are produced. | 1607–1608

Cymbeline is produced. | 1609–1610

The Winter's Tale is produced. | 1610–1611

The Tempest is produced. | 1611

The Famous History of the Life of Henry the Eighth is produced. | 1612–1613

Shakespeare collaborates with John Fletcher to write *The Two Noble Kinsmen*. | 1613

Shakespeare dies and is buried in Holy Trinity Church in Stratford-upon-Avon. | April 23, 1616

A Midsummer Night's Dream

The Renaissance in England

The word *renaissance* means, literally, "rebirth." Historians use the word to refer to the period between the fifteenth and early seventeenth centuries when Europe was influenced by a rebirth of interest in Greek and Latin learning. This renewal of interest in classical learning and literature moved Europeans from medieval habits of thought toward more modern habits.

Rediscovering the arts and literature of classical Greece and Rome brought about, first in Italy and then in the rest of Europe, a renewed interest in human life on earth. The Renaissance devotion to Greek and Latin classics has thus become known as Humanism. Many Humanist philosophers believed that human beings were created in the image of God and that each person was a little world, or *microcosmos,* complete in himself or herself. They believed that humans, sharing as they did in the divine, could perfect themselves and the institutions of this world. Out of this belief came a new emphasis on learning and on the arts, as well as religious and political debates that led to the Protestant Reformation, the decline of feudalism, and the emergence of modern nationalism. Also, the invention of the printing press in 1453 allowed information to spread more quickly and encouraged people to read, to write, to think for themselves, and to challenge authority.

In England, the period from 1558 to 1603 is known as the Elizabethan Age after Elizabeth I, the queen who reigned during this period. English literature reached what many people consider to be its zenith during the Elizabethan Age. Shakespeare wrote and produced his plays at the height of the Elizabethan period and throughout much of the Jacobean period, the period from 1603 to 1625 when James I ruled England.

Shakespeare's writing is a good example of the spirit of the Renaissance—his plays often focus on memorable and complex characters, his plots often are derived from classical sources, and his themes often involve challenges to authority. Although Shakespeare's scholarly contemporary and fellow playwright Ben Jonson wrote of Shakespeare, "thou hadst small Latin, and less Greek," Shakespeare knew far more of these languages than most people do today, and he probably read many of the classical works of Rome in their original Latin. Play writing in Shakespeare's time was not so much a matter of inventing a subject and characters previously unknown to the stage as it was a process of adapting, alluding to, and drawing inspiration from both classical and contemporary sources. Shakespeare was inspired by classical works and by the history of Rome to write such plays as *The Tragedy of Julius Cæsar, The Tragedy of Antony and Cleopatra,* and *The Tragedy of Coriolanus.* While the plots of these plays are derived from classical sources, Shakespeare also was inspired by and reworked the stories and plays of his contemporaries to produce *The Tragedy of Romeo and Juliet, As You Like It,* and other plays. Shakespeare also developed his own plots for which no source is known in plays like *A Midsummer Night's Dream* and *The Tempest.* Even these works, however, are filled with classical and contemporary allusions.

Types of Renaissance Drama

The two most common types of drama during the English Renaissance were comedies and tragedies. The key difference between comedies and tragedies is that the former have happy endings and the latter unhappy. It is only a slight exaggeration to say that Renaissance comedies end with wedding bells and tragedies with funeral bells.

A **comedy** is typically lighthearted, though it may contain serious action and themes. Action in a comedy usually progresses from initial order to a humorous misunderstanding or confusion and back to order again. Stock elements of comedy include mistaken identities, puns and word play, and coarse or exaggerated characters. Shakespeare's comedies frequently lead to one or more marriages.

A **tragedy** tells the story of the downfall of a person of high status. Often it celebrates the courage and dignity of its hero in the face of inevitable doom. The hero is typically neither completely good nor completely evil but lives and acts between these extremes. The hero's fall may be brought about by some flaw in his or her character, known as a **tragic flaw.**

Another kind of popular play produced during this period was the **history**, or play about events from the past. Shakespeare frequently used elements of tragedy in his histories, although some of his histories also include comic elements. In Renaissance England, **masques** were also popular. These were elaborate shows that featured acting, music, and dance. The actors were often lavishly costumed and masked. Masques were popular in the courts of Elizabeth I and James I, and their theme was often an allegorical or mythological compliment to the noble or group of nobles for whom they were performed. Shakespeare often included in his plays such elements of masques as processions or masked dances.

Four of Shakespeare's late plays—*Pericles, Prince of Tyre; Cymbeline; The Winter's Tale;* and *The Tempest*—that were originally classified as comedies have been reclassified as romances by later scholars. **Romances** are theatrical and nonrealistic. They frequently employ fantastic elements like fairies and magical spells. They combine comic and tragic themes, and contain plots that move towards reunion, reconciliation, and regeneration. Standard devices in romances include music and song; the changing of old garments for fresh ones to signify transformation; and startling spectacles, or surprising and visually striking scenes—such as the reunion of characters who believed each other to be dead—that inspire the audience to question the relationship between reality and illusion.

The Political Conditions of Theater in Renaissance London

In the late sixteenth century, London was a bustling city of perhaps 150,000 people—the mercantile, political, and artistic center of England. The city proper was ruled by a mayor and aldermen who frowned upon theater because it brought together large crowds of people, creating the potential for lawlessness and the spread of controversial ideas and disease. Many times, London city officials or Parliament ordered the theaters closed, once because they objected to the political content of a play called *Isle of Dogs,* and regularly because of outbreaks of plague. Parliament, which was dominated by Puritans, passed laws that made it possible for traveling actors and other performers to be arrested as vagabonds and cruelly punished. For protection, actors sought the patronage of members of the nobility. Actors would become, technically, servants of a famous lord, and troupes went by such names as The Lord Worcester's Men. Fortunately for actors and playwrights, Queen Elizabeth and other members of the nobility loved the theater and pro-tected it. Elizabeth herself maintained two troupes of boy actors, connected to her royal chapels. In addition to such troupes, London boasted several professional troupes made up of men. In those days, women did not act, and women's roles were played by men, a fact that further increased Puritan disapproval of the theaters. When the Puritans took control of England in 1642, theater was banned altogether.

The Renaissance Playhouse

In 1576, James Burbage built the first professional play-house in England. Burbage located his playhouse, which he called simply the Theater, just outside the northern bound-aries of the City of London, where he could avoid control by city authorities. Another professional theater, the Curtain, was built nearby shortly thereafter. In 1599, Burbage's son Richard and other members of Chamberlain's Men tore down the Theater and used its materials to build a new play-house, the Globe Theater, south of the city on the banks of the river Thames. One of the shareholders in the Globe was William Shakespeare.

From contemporary drawings and descriptions and from evidence in plays, we can reconstruct what Shakespeare's Globe must have looked like. The building was octagonal, or eight-sided, its inner walls holding galleries covered by peaked, thatched roofs (see illustration, next page). The cen-ter of this "wooden O," as Shakespeare called it, was open to the air. The stage projected into the middle of this open space, and poorer theatergoers called "groundlings," who paid a penny apiece for admission, stood around three sides of the stage. Wealthier playgoers could pay an additional penny or two to sit in one of the three galleries set in the walls of the theater. In many respects, the theater was simi-lar to medieval stages—a wagon pulled into the open court-yard of an inn, with the inn's balconies around it.

The stage itself was partially covered by a canopy supported by two large pillars. Trapdoors in the stage floor allowed for appearances by spirits or fairies and for the disappearance of bodies. Behind the stage, between the pillars, was an inner area called the "tiring house" that could be used for changing costumes and for indoor scenes such as throne rooms, bed-chambers, and taverns. On either side of the rear of the stage were doors for entrances and exits. At the back of the tiring house was a door and stairway that led to a second-level play-ing area that could be used as a hilltop, a castle turret, or a

balcony (perhaps for the famous balcony scene from *Romeo and Juliet*). On the third level, above this balcony area, was an area for musicians and sound effects people. A cannon shot from this area during a performance of Shakespeare's *Henry the Eighth* in 1613 caused a fire that burned the Globe to the ground.

Because the playhouse was open to the air, plays were presented in the daytime, and there was little or no artificial lighting. Scenery in the modern sense was nonexistent, and very few properties were used, beyond an occasional table or chair. Audiences had to use their imaginations to create the scenes, and playwrights helped their audiences to do this by writing descriptions of scenes into their characters' speeches.

The Renaissance Audience

Audiences at the Globe and similar theaters were quite heterogeneous, or mixed. They included people from all stations of society: laboring people from the lower classes, middle-class merchants, members of Parliament, and lords and ladies. Pickpockets mingled among the noisy, raucous groundlings crowded around the stage. Noble men and women sat on cushioned seats in the first-tier balcony. The fanfare of trumpets that signaled the beginning of a play was heard by some twenty-five hundred people, a cross section of the Elizabethan world. That Shakespeare's plays have such universal appeal may be explained by this fact: they were written for everyone, from "the most able, to him that can but spell."

A Midsummer Night's Dream in Context

Shakespeare probably wrote *A Midsummer Night's Dream* in 1595, a year in which he was likely excited by the reopening of the theaters (they had closed due to an outbreak of plague in 1593). At this time, Shakespeare was reaching his height as a writer of dramatic comedies and was writing his first major tragedy, *The Tragedy of Romeo and Juliet.* Many believe that *A Midsummer Night's Dream* is Shakespeare's finest comedy, revealing his fertile imagination at its best. Like most comedies of his day, the play centers around romantic relationships leading to marriage and derives much of its humor from the mishaps and misunderstandings the young couples experience before their romantic relationships are sorted out. The play draws its strength, however, not from the conventional story of young people hoping to find true love, but from the rich contrasts in the Athens of Shakespeare's imagination. There, Theseus, duke of Athens, rules and carries out the letter of the law in the city while mischievous fairies rule a kingdom of their own in the wild forest just outside the city. The story offers a wide array of characters: from the mischievous fairies to the witty noblemen and women, from unreasonable fathers to bumbling craftsmen. It is a place where identity itself is uncertain—in order to find their destiny the characters must essentially lose themselves for a time. It is a story of song, airy charm, and broad slapstick.

Like most playwrights of his period and writers throughout time, Shakespeare was a great borrower from the works of others, those of antiquity and his contemporaries. While Shakespeare adapted many of his plots from known sources, there is no identifiable source for *A Midsummer Night's Dream* as a whole. Shakespeare may have drawn the theme of transformation and the story of Pyramus and Thisbe from Ovid's *Metamorphoses* (see Selections for Additional Reading, page 99). Shakespeare, however, made original use of the classical Pyramus and Thisbe story—as subject matter not for tragedy but for farce. Theseus and Hippolyta may have been modeled on Geoffrey Chaucer's characters in "The Knight's Tale" of his famous *Canterbury Tales.* Shakespeare was also familiar with Plutarch's *Lives of The Noble Grecians and Romans,* which features Theseus and Hippolyta. While *A Midsummer Night's Dream* is set in classical Athens and there are many classical references, some critics argue that both Theseus and Athens seem to belong more to Chaucer's medieval period than to Plutarch's classical period. Shakespeare also drew inspiration for *A Midsummer Night's Dream* from the superstitions and folk traditions of the English countryside that he knew so well. Stories about fairies abounded in rural England, and country people told stories about the mischievous wood sprite Robin Goodfellow, a character whom Shakespeare transplanted to the woods outside Athens. Shakespeare also included elements of May Day festivals and the festivities of Midsummer's Eve, a celebration held on the shortest night of the year, June 23. In the title of his work, Shakespeare also alludes to the folk belief in "midsummer madness," a condition in which a person experiences imaginative delusions brought on by the heat of summer.

Many critics have speculated that *A Midsummer Night's Dream* was written and performed to celebrate an aristocratic wedding, and, indeed, there is much in the play to support such speculation. Its subject matter and themes would have been appropriate for a court wedding, and some have theorized that certain passages may have been intended as compliments to Queen Elizabeth. The play shares many elements with the court masque, a form of entertainment popular among the aristocracy of the period and characterized by music, song, dance, and fanciful characters. The play also contains an element of the masque made popular by Shakespeare's contemporary and rival dramatist Ben Jonson—the antimasque. An antimasque, a burlesque comic sketch, took place before the masque itself, and the antimasque's grotesque elements were meant to contrast with the sophistication and elegance of the masque. With his customary ingenuity, however, Shakespeare places what can be considered his antimasque—the artisans' presentation of the Pyramus and Thisbe story—at the end of *A Midsummer Night's Dream,* where it serves to comment on the action of the play as a whole.

Nevertheless, *A Midsummer Night's Dream* is much richer and broader in focus than any court masque. It raises questions about the difference between art and life, the theater and the everyday world, the dreaming and the waking world. Its characters are drawn not only from the nobility but from the common class, and while the "low" characters in the play—Bottom, Quince, Flute, and the other artisans— are burlesqued, their self-knowledge and kindliness often stands in contrast to the behavior of the nobles. Also, Bottom, a mere commoner, is the only human character in the play allowed to glimpse and directly interact with the third group of characters in the play—the fairies. Thus, in *A Midsummer Night's Dream*, Shakespeare creates three separate but very interdependent worlds—the witty world of the aristocracy, the coarse humor of the well-meaning artisans, and the supernatural world of the fairies—for the audience to take delight in, compare and contrast, and view critically.

The play was written about the same time as one of Shakespeare's first and finest tragedies, *The Tragedy of Romeo and Juliet*. The two plays share character types—heedless, young couples in love, tyrannical fathers who attempt to separate young couples, and remote rulers who are unable to understand the power of young love. Many critics have argued that *A Midsummer Night's Dream* is the flip side of *The Tragedy of Romeo and Juliet*. In *The Tragedy of Romeo and Juliet*, love leads to disaster. In *A Midsummer Night's Dream*, love leads to joy and marriage, but only after narrowly averting tragedy. Indeed, even the tragic consequences to which young love may lead are mocked in *A Midsummer Night's Dream* in the presentation of the Pyramus and Thisbe story.

While *A Midsummer Night's Dream* was most likely well received by the aristocratic audience for whom some have suggested it was written and performed, it was not one of Shakespeare's most popular plays among his general audience. From the time of Shakespeare's death until the twentieth century, the play was seen as one of Shakespeare's lesser works and as a silly bit of fantasy. Modern audiences have rediscovered the richness and complexity of *A Midsummer Night's Dream*. Indeed, some of its major themes—the magical journey from a civilized place to a wild place and back again, as well as the idea that sometimes it is necessary to lose yourself in order to find yourself—have influenced many modern works of literature and film.

Echoes

All the world's a stage,
And all the men and women merely players;
They have their exits and their entrances,
And one man in his time plays many parts.

—As You Like It

Our revels now are ended. These our actors
(As I foretold you) were all spirits, and
Are melted into air, into thin air,
And like the baseless fabric of this vision,
The cloud-capp'd tow'rs, the gorgeous palaces,
The solemn temples, the great globe itself,
Yea, all which it inherit, shall dissolve,
And like this insubstantial pageant faded
Leave not a rack behind. We are such stuff
As dreams are made on; and our little life
Is rounded with a sleep.

—The Tempest

O for a Muse of fire, that would ascend
The brightest heaven of invention!
A kingdom for a stage, princes to act,
And monarchs to behold the swelling scene!
Then should the warlike Harry, like himself,
Assume the port of Mars, and at his heels
(Leash'd in, like hounds) should famine, sword, and fire
Crouch for employment. But pardon, gentles all,
The flat unraised spirits that hath dar'd
On this unworthy scaffold to bring forth
So great an object. Can this cockpit hold
The vasty fields of France? Or may we cram
Within this wooden O the very casques
That did affright the air at Agincourt?
O, pardon! since a crooked figure may
Attest in little place a million,
And let us, ciphers to this great accompt,
On your imaginary forces work.

—The Life of Henry the Fifth

ILLUSTRATION **xix**

Dramatis Personae

THESEUS, *Duke of Athens*

EGEUS, *father to Hermia*

LYSANDER
DEMETRIUS } *in love with Hermia*

PHILOSTRATE, *Master of the Revels to Theseus*

QUINCE, *a carpenter*
BOTTOM, *a weaver*
FLUTE, *a bellows-mender*
SNOUT, *a tinker*
SNUG, *a joiner*
STARVELING, *a tailor* } *presenting* { PROLOGUE
PYRAMUS
THISBY[1]
WALL
LION
MOONSHINE

HIPPOLYTA, *Queen of the Amazons, betrothed to Theseus*

HERMIA, *daughter to Egeus, in love with Lysander*

HELENA, *in love with Demetrius*

OBERON, *King of the Fairies*

TITANIA, *Queen of the Fairies*

PUCK, *or* ROBIN GOODFELLOW

PEASEBLOSSOM
COBWEB
MOTH
MUSTARDSEED } *fairies*

Other FAIRIES *attending their King and Queen;* ATTENDANTS *on Theseus and Hippolyta*

SCENE: *Athens, and a wood near it.*

---

1. THISBY. Shakespeare's spelling of Thisbe

Act I

SCENE i: Athens. The palace of Theseus.

Enter THESEUS, HIPPOLYTA, PHILOSTRATE, *with* OTHERS.

THESEUS. Now, fair Hippolyta, our <u>nuptial</u> hour
Draws on apace. Four happy days bring in
Another moon; but, methinks, how slow
This old moon wanes! She lingers[1] my desires,
5 Like to a stepdame, or a dowager,[2]
Long withering out a young man's revenue.[3]

HIPPOLYTA. Four days will quickly <u>steep</u> themselves in
    night;
Four nights will quickly dream away the time;
And then the moon, like to a silver bow
10 New bent in heaven, shall behold the night
Of our solemnities.[4]

THESEUS.   Go, Philostrate,
Stir up the Athenian youth to merriments,
Awake the <u>pert</u> and nimble spirit of mirth,
Turn melancholy forth to funerals;
15 The pale companion[5] is not for our pomp.[6]

                         Exit PHILOSTRATE.

Hippolyta, I woo'd thee with my sword,
And won thy love doing thee injuries;[7]
But I will wed thee in another key,
With pomp, with triumph,[8] and with reveling.

Enter EGEUS *and his daughter* HERMIA *and* LYSANDER *and*
DEMETRIUS.

20 EGEUS. Happy be Theseus, our renowned Duke!

◄ For what event is
Theseus waiting?
How does he feel
about this upcoming
event?

◄ Under what cir-
cumstances did
Theseus and
Hippolyta meet?
What does Theseus
promise?

ACT I, SCENE i
  1. **lingers.** Is unnecessarily slow in fulfilling
  2. **stepdame . . . dowager.** *Stepdame*—stepmother; *dowager*—widow with the
title or property of her dead husband
  3. **withering out a young man's revenue.** Draining a young man's money
because she (the stepdame or dowager) requires support
  4. **solemnities.** Solemn ceremony or ritual; here, referring to Theseus and
Hippolyta's wedding ceremony
  5. **companion.** Fellow, here used contemptuously
  6. **pomp.** Stately, brilliant, or ceremonial display or pageant
  7. **Hippolyta . . . injuries.** Theseus had conquered the Amazons in battle and
had captured and taken captive Hippolyta, the Amazon queen.
  8. **triumph.** Public spectacle, procession, or celebration

Words For Everyday Use	nup • tial (nup′shəl) *adj.*, of marriage or a wedding
	steep (stēp) *vt.*, immerse, saturate, absorb, or imbue
	pert (purt) *adj.*, lively, jaunty

THESEUS. Thanks, good Egeus. What's the news with thee?

EGEUS. Full of <u>vexation</u> come I, with complaint
Against my child, my daughter Hermia.
Stand forth, Demetrius. My noble lord,
25 This man hath my consent to marry her.
Stand forth, Lysander. And, my gracious Duke,
This man hath bewitch'd the bosom of my child.
Thou, thou, Lysander, thou hast given her rhymes,
And interchang'd love-tokens with my child;
30 Thou hast by moonlight at her window sung
With faining voice verses of faining love,[9]
And stol'n the impression of her fantasy[10]
With bracelets of thy hair, rings, gawds, conceits,
Knacks, trifles, nosegays, sweetmeats[11]—messengers
35 Of strong prevailment in unhardened youth.
With cunning hast thou <u>filch'd</u> my daughter's heart,
Turn'd her obedience (which is due to me)
To stubborn harshness. And, my gracious Duke,
Be it so she will not here before your Grace
40 Consent to marry with Demetrius,
I beg the ancient privilege of Athens:
As she is mine, I may dispose of her;
Which shall be either to this gentleman,
Or to her death, according to our law
45 Immediately[12] provided in that case.

THESEUS. What say you, Hermia? Be advis'd, fair maid.
To you your father should be as a god;
One that compos'd your beauties; yea, and one
To whom you are but as a form in wax,
50 By him imprinted, and within his power,
To leave the figure, or disfigure[13] it.
Demetrius is a worthy gentleman.

► With whom is Egeus angry? What does he wish his daughter to do? Of what does he accuse Lysander?

► What has Lysander done to win Hermia's heart?

► What does Egeus demand of Theseus? What law exists in Athens?

► How does Theseus say Hermia should view her father? What does he warn Hermia her father has the power to do?

---

9. **faining . . . love.** *Faining voice*—loving voice; fabricating, pretending voice; *faining love*—glad, ready love; invented, simulated love
10. **stol'n the impression of her fantasy.** Impressed your image on her imagination; made her fall in love with you
11. **bracelets of thy hair . . . sweetmeats.** Young people in this period sometimes gave their beloved a bracelet made of their own hair; "gawds, conceits, / Knacks, trifles" refers to trinkets and knickknacks; nosegays are small bouquets of flowers; and sweetmeats are any sweet food prepared with sugar or honey.
12. **Immediately.** Expressly; for the specific purpose
13. **disfigure.** Completely destroy; obliterate

| Words For Everyday Use | **vex • a • tion** (veks ā´shən) *n.*, irritation, aggravation |
| | **filch** (filch) *vt.*, steal |

HERMIA. So is Lysander.

THESEUS.   In himself he is;
But in this kind, wanting your father's voice,[14]
55   The other must be held the worthier.

HERMIA. I would my father look'd but with my eyes.

THESEUS. Rather your eyes must with his judgment look.

HERMIA. I do <u>entreat</u> your Grace to pardon me.
I know not by what power I am made bold,
60   Nor how it may concern my modesty,
In such a presence here to plead my thoughts;
But I beseech your Grace that I may know
The worst that may befall me in this case,
If I refuse to wed Demetrius.

65   THESEUS. Either to die the death,[15] or to abjure
For ever the society of men.
Therefore, fair Hermia, question your desires,
Know of your youth, examine well your blood,[16]
Whether (if you yield not to your father's choice)
70   You can <u>endure</u> the <u>livery</u> of a nun,
For aye to be in shady <u>cloister</u> mew'd,[17]
To live a <u>barren</u> sister all your life,
Chanting faint hymns to the cold fruitless moon.[18]
Thrice blessed they that master so their blood
75   To undergo such maiden pilgrimage;
But earthlier happy is the rose distill'd,[19]
Than that which withering on the virgin thorn
Grows, lives, and dies in single blessedness.

HERMIA. So will I grow, so live, so die, my lord,
80   <u>Ere I will yield my virgin patent</u>[20] up
Unto his lordship, whose unwished yoke
My soul consents not to give <u>sovereignty</u>.

THESEUS. Take time to pause, and by the next new moon—
The sealing-day betwixt my love and me

What will happen to Hermia should she persist in her refusal to marry Demetrius?

According to Theseus, what are the advantages and disadvantages of becoming a nun?

What is Hermia's decision?

What are Hermia's only three options? On what day must she give her final decision?

14. **But . . . voice.** But in this particular respect, lacking your father's approval
15. **die the death.** Be put to death according to the law
16. **Know . . . blood.** Examine youthful feelings and passions
17. **mew'd.** Caged; confined
18. **cold fruitless moon.** Artemis (or to the Romans, Diana), virgin moon goddess
19. **distill'd.** Made into perfume
20. **patent.** Privilege

Words For Everyday Use

en • treat (en trēt´) vt., beg; beseech
en • dure (en door´) vt., bear, tolerate
liv • er • y (liv´ər ē) n., uniform

clois • ter (klois´tər) n., convent
bar • ren (bar´ən) adj., sterile
sov • er • eign • ty (säv´rən tē) n., the status or dominion of a ruler

85 For everlasting bond of fellowship—
Upon that day either prepare to die
For disobedience to your father's will,
Or else to wed Demetrius, as he would,
Or on Diana's altar to protest[21]
90 For aye[22] <u>austerity</u> and single life.

DEMETRIUS. Relent, sweet Hermia, and, Lysander, yield
Thy crazed title[23] to my certain right.

LYSANDER. You have her father's love, Demetrius,
Let me have Hermia's; do you marry him.

95 EGEUS. Scornful Lysander, true, he hath my love;
And what is mine, my love shall render him.
And she is mine, and all my right of her
I do estate unto[24] Demetrius.

LYSANDER. I am, my lord, as well <u>deriv'd</u>[25] as he,
100 As well possess'd;[26] my love is more than his;
My fortunes every way as fairly rank'd
(If not with vantage) as Demetrius';
And (which is more than all these boasts can be)
I am belov'd of beauteous Hermia.
105 Why should not I then prosecute my right?
Demetrius, I'll avouch it to his head,[27]
Made love to Nedar's daughter, Helena,
And won her soul, and she, sweet lady, <u>dotes</u>,
Devoutly dotes, dotes in <u>idolatry</u>,
110 Upon this spotted[28] and <u>inconstant</u> man.

THESEUS. I must confess that I have heard so much,
And with Demetrius thought to have spoke thereof;
But, being over-full of self-affairs,
My mind did lose it. But, Demetrius, come,
115 And come, Egeus, you shall go with me;
I have some private schooling for you both.
For you, fair Hermia, look you arm yourself

---

21. **protest.** Affirm solemnly; vow
22. **For aye.** Forever
23. **crazed title.** False claim
24. **estate unto.** Bestow upon
25. **deriv'd.** Born
26. **well possess'd.** Wealthy
27. **avouch it to his head.** Declare it to his face
28. **spotted.** Morally blemished

Words For Everyday Use

aus • ter • i • ty (ô ster´ə tē) *n.*, state of severe plainness and simplicity
dote (dōt) *vi.*, be excessively fond

i • dol • a • try (ī däl´ə trē) *n.*, excessive devotion to a person or thing
in • con • stant (in kän´stənt) *adj.*, fickle; unsteady in affections

To fit your fancies to your father's will;
Or else the law of Athens yields you up

120 (Which by no means we may extenuate)
To death, or to a vow of single life.
Come, my Hippolyta; what cheer, my love?
Demetrius and Egeus, go along;
I must employ you in some business

125 Against[29] our nuptial, and confer with you
Of something nearly[30] that concerns yourselves.

EGEUS. With duty and desire we follow you.

Exeunt. Manent[31] LYSANDER *and* HERMIA.

LYSANDER. How now, my love? why is your cheek so
pale?
How chance the roses there do fade so fast?

130 HERMIA. Belike[32] for want of rain; which I could well
Beteem[33] them from the tempest of my eyes.

LYSANDER. Ay me! for aught[34] that I could ever read,
Could ever hear by tale or history,
The course of true love never did run smooth;

135 But either it was different in blood—

HERMIA. O cross! too high to be enthrall'd[35] to low.

LYSANDER. Or else misgraffed[36] in respect of years—

HERMIA. O spite! too old to be engag'd to young.

LYSANDER. Or else it stood upon the choice of friends—

140 HERMIA. O hell, to choose love by another's eyes!

LYSANDER. Or if there were a sympathy in choice,
War, death, or sickness did lay siege to it,
Making it momentany[37] as a sound,
Swift as a shadow, short as any dream,

145 Brief as the lightning in the collied[38] night,
That, in a spleen,[39] unfolds both heaven and earth;
And ere[40] a man hath power to say "Behold!"

◄ What does
Theseus claim he is
unable to do?

◄ What have tales
and history taught
Lysander about love?

◄ According to
Lysander, what
happens to a rela-
tionship even if two
people love each
other?

---

29. **Against.** In preparation for
30. **nearly.** Closely
31. *Exeunt. Manent.* They exit. Remain
32. **Belike.** Quite likely
33. **Beteem.** Bring forth; pour out for them
34. **aught.** All
35. **enthrall'd.** Enslaved
36. **misgraffed.** Poorly matched
37. **momentany.** Momentary
38. **collied.** Blackened, as if with coal
39. **spleen.** Flash or fit of passion
40. **ere.** Before

The jaws of darkness do devour it up:
So quick bright things come to confusion.

150 HERMIA. If then true lovers have been ever cross'd
It stands as an <u>edict</u> in destiny.
Then let us teach our trial patience,[41]
Because it is a customary cross,
As due to love as thoughts and dreams and sighs,
155 Wishes and tears, poor fancy's[42] followers.

LYSANDER. A good persuasion;[43] therefore hear me,
    Hermia.
I have a widow aunt, a dowager,
Of great revenue, and she hath no child.
From Athens is her house remote seven leagues;
160 And she respects me as her only son.
There, gentle Hermia, may I marry thee;
And to that place the sharp Athenian law
Cannot pursue us. If thou lovest me, then
Steal forth thy father's house tomorrow night;
165 And in the wood, a league without the town
(Where I did meet thee once with Helena
To do observance to a morn of May),[44]
There will I stay for thee.

HERMIA.   My good Lysander,
I swear to thee, by Cupid's strongest bow,
170 By his best arrow with the golden head,[45]
By the simplicity of Venus' doves,
By that which knitteth souls and prospers loves,
And by that fire which burn'd the Carthage queen[46]
When the false Troyan under sail was seen,
175 By all the vows that ever men have broke
(In number more than ever women spoke),
In that same place thou hast appointed me
Tomorrow truly will I meet with thee.

► What plan to escape Athenian law has Lysander devised? Where does he plan to meet Hermia to carry out this plan?

---

41. **teach . . . patience.** Teach ourselves to bear out trials, or difficulties, patiently
42. **fancy's.** Love's
43. **persuasion.** Conviction; strong belief
44. **To . . . May.** To observe and participate in a May Day ceremony
45. **arrow. . . head.** It was believed that Cupid's gold-tipped arrows caused people to fall in love, while his lead-tipped arrows caused people to feel dislike.
46. **Carthage queen.** Dido, queen of Carthage, ended her life by burning herself on a funeral pyre after her beloved Aeneas, a Trojan, left her to sail for Italy.

Words
For
Everyday
Use

e • dict (ē'dikt') *n.*, official public proclamation or order issued by authority; decree

LYSANDER. Keep promise, love. Look, here comes Helena.

Enter HELENA.

180 **HERMIA.** God speed fair Helena! whither away?

HELENA. Call you me fair?[47] That fair again unsay.
Demetrius loves your fair, O happy fair!
Your eyes are lodestars,[48] and your tongue's sweet air[49]
More tuneable than lark to shepherd's ear
185 When wheat is green, when hawthorn buds appear.
Sickness is catching; O, were favor[50] so,
Yours would I catch, fair Hermia, ere I go;
My ear should catch your voice, my eye your eye,
My tongue should catch your tongue's sweet melody.
190 Were the world mine, Demetrius being bated,[51]
The rest I'll give to be to you translated.
O, teach me how you look, and with what art
You sway the motion of Demetrius' heart.

HERMIA. I frown upon him; yet he loves me still.

195 **HELENA.** O that your frowns would teach my smiles such skill!

HERMIA. I give him curses; yet he gives me love.

HELENA. O that my prayers could such affection move!

HERMIA. The more I hate, the more he follows me.

HELENA. The more I love, the more he hateth me.

200 **HERMIA.** His folly, Helena, is no fault of mine.

HELENA. None but your beauty; would that fault were mine!

HERMIA. Take comfort; he no more shall see my face
Lysander and myself will fly this place.
Before the time I did Lysander see,
205 Seem'd Athens as a paradise to me:
O then, what graces in my love do dwell,
That he hath turn'd a heaven unto a hell!

LYSANDER. Helen, to you our minds we will unfold:
Tomorrow night, when Phoebe[52] doth behold

◄ *Why is Helena unhappy with her appearance? Why does she wish to be just like Hermia?*

---

47. **fair.** While *fair* means "beauty," in this context it also refers to Helena's blonde coloring which she says Demetrius has rejected in favor of Hermia's dark beauty.
48. **lodestars.** Guiding stars
49. **air.** Music
50. **favor.** Physical appearance; facial features
51. **bated.** Excepted
52. **Phoebe.** Another name for Artemis, or Diana, goddess of the moon

210 Her silver <u>visage</u> in the wat'ry glass,
Decking with liquid pearl the bladed grass
(A time that lovers' flights doth still[53] conceal),
Through Athens' gates have we <u>devis'd</u> to steal.

► What relationship
exists between
Hermia and Helena?

HERMIA. And in the wood, where often you and I
215 Upon faint primrose beds were wont to lie,
Emptying our bosoms of their counsel[54] sweet,
There my Lysander and myself shall meet;
And thence from Athens turn away our eyes,
To seek new friends and stranger companies.[55]
220 Farewell, sweet playfellow, pray thou for us;
And good luck grant thee thy Demetrius!
Keep word, Lysander; we must starve our sight
From lovers' food[56] till morrow deep midnight.

LYSANDER. I will, my Hermia.   *Exit* HERMIA.

                                        Helena, adieu:
225 As you on him, Demetrius dote on you!

                                        Exit LYSANDER.

HELENA. How happy some o'er other some[57] can be!
Through Athens I am thought as fair as she.
But what of that? Demetrius thinks not so
He will not know what all but he do know,
230 And as he errs, doting on Hermia's eyes,
So I, admiring of his qualities.
Things base and vile, holding no quantity,[58]
Love can transpose to form and dignity.
Love looks not with the eyes but with the mind;

► What does Helena
say about love?

235 And therefore is wing'd Cupid painted blind.
Nor hath Love's mind of any judgment taste;
Wings, and no eyes, figure[59] unheedy haste
And therefore is Love said to be a child,
Because in choice he is so oft <u>beguil'd</u>.
240 As <u>waggish</u> boys in game themselves <u>forswear</u>,

---

53. **still.** Always
54. **counsel.** Inner thoughts; secrets
55. **stranger companies.** Company of strangers
56. **we . . . food.** We must not see each other
57. **some o'er other some.** Some more than others
58. **holding no quantity.** Unshapely; unattractive
59. **figure.** Represent

Words For Everyday Use	vis • age (vĭz´ij) *n.*, face de • vise (di vīz´) *vt.*, contrive; plan be • guile (bē gīl´) *vt.*, deceive; charm	wag • gish (wag´ish) *adj.*, roguishly merry for • swear (fôr swer´) *vt.*, renounce an oath; swear falsely

So the boy Love is perjur'd every where;
For ere Demetrius look'd on Hermia's eyne,[60]
He hail'd down oaths that he was only mine
And when this hail some heat from Hermia felt,
245 So he dissolv'd, and show'rs of oaths did melt.
I will go tell him of fair Hermia's flight;
Then to the wood will he tomorrow night
Pursue her; and for this intelligence[61]
If I have thanks, it is a dear expense.
250 But herein mean I to enrich my pain,
To have his sight thither and back again.   *Exit.*

◄ *What does Helena plan to do? Why?*

SCENE ii: Quince's house.

Enter QUINCE *the carpenter and* SNUG *the joiner and* BOTTOM *the weaver and* FLUTE *the bellowsmender and* SNOUT *the tinker and* STARVELING *the tailor.*[1]

QUINCE. Is all our company here?

BOTTOM. You were best to call them generally,[2] man by man, according to the scrip.

QUINCE. Here is the scroll of every man's name which is
5 thought fit, through all Athens, to play in our enterlude[3] before the Duke and the Duchess, on his wedding day at night.

◄ *What is this group of people planning on doing?*

BOTTOM. First, good Peter Quince, say what the play treats on; then read the names of the actors; and so
10 grow to a point.

QUINCE. Marry,[4] our play is *The most lamentable comedy and most cruel death of Pyramus and Thisby.*

◄ *What play do they wish to perform? What happens to Pyramus and Thisby in this play? What is Bottom's assessment of this "piece of work"?*

BOTTOM. A very good piece of work, I assure you, and a merry. Now, good Peter Quince, call forth your actors by
15 the scroll. Masters, spread yourselves.

---

60. **eyne.** Eyes
61. **intelligence.** Information
ACT I, SCENE ii
   1. QUINCE . . . *tailor.* The names of all the craftsmen are derived from their trade; Quince's name comes from an old name for a wedge carpenters use; Snug's name means "close fit," a property joints must have; Bottom's name is the trim for the tool on which weavers wind their thread; Flute's name refers to the stops of an organ, which bellows menders also repaired; Snout refers to the nose or spout of a teapot, which tinkers repaired; and Starveling's name is derived from a proverb about the thinness of tailors.
   2. **generally.** Bottom means "individually"; occasionally he mistakenly says the exact opposite of what he means.
   3. **enterlude.** Interlude; short dramatic entertainment
   4. **Marry.** Interjection derived from "By the Virgin Mary," originally an oath

▶ What role is
Bottom to play?

QUINCE. Answer as I call you. Nick Bottom the weaver.

BOTTOM. Ready. Name what part I am for, and proceed.

QUINCE. You, Nick Bottom, are set down for Pyramus.

BOTTOM. What is Pyramus? a lover, or a tyrant?

20 QUINCE. A lover, that kills himself most gallant for love.

▶ What does
Bottom say he will
do in his role as
Pyramus? What type
of role would he
really like to play?

BOTTOM. That will ask some tears in the true performing of it. If I do it, let the audience look to their eyes. I will move storms; I will condole[5] in some measure. To the rest—yet my chief humor is for a tyrant. I could play

25 Ercles[6] rarely, or a part to tear a cat[7] in, to make all split.

"The raging rocks
And shivering shocks
shall break the locks
Of prison gates;

30 And Phibbus' car[8]
Shall shine from far,
And make and <u>mar</u>
The foolish Fates."

This was lofty! Now name the rest of the players. This is

35 Ercles' vein, a tyrant's vein, a lover is more condoling.

QUINCE. Francis Flute the bellows-mender.

FLUTE. Here, Peter Quince.

QUINCE. Flute, you must take Thisby on you.

FLUTE. What is Thisby? a wand'ring knight?

▶ Whom is Flute to
play? Why doesn't
he want to play this
role?

40 QUINCE. It is the lady that Pyramus must love.

FLUTE. Nay, faith; let not me play a woman; I have a beard coming.[9]

QUINCE. That's all one; you shall play it in a mask, and you may speak as small[10] as you will.

---

5. **condole.** Express sympathy; arouse pity
6. **Ercles.** Hercules
7. **tear a cat.** Rant and roar
8. **Phibbus' car.** Mistaken pronunciation of Phoebus, whom the ancients believed drove a chariot which they identified with the sun
9. **let . . . coming.** In Shakespeare's day, boys played female roles in the theater; Flute is protesting that he is too old to play a woman.
10. **small.** Gently, softly

| Words For Everyday Use | mar (mär) *vt.*, injure or damage |

45   **BOTTOM.** And I may hide my face, let me play Thisby too. I'll speak in a monstrous little voice, "Thisne! Thisne! Ah, Pyramus, my lover dear! thy Thisby dear, and lady dear!"

◄ *What does Bottom wish to do?*

   QUINCE. No, no, you must play Pyramus; and, Flute,
50   you Thisby.

   BOTTOM. Well, proceed.

   QUINCE. Robin Starveling the tailor.

   STARVELING. Here, Peter Quince.

   QUINCE. Robin Starveling, you must play Thisby's
55   mother. Tom Snout the tinker.

   SNOUT. Here, Peter Quince.

   QUINCE. You, Pyramus' father; myself, Thisby's father; Snug the joiner, you the lion's part. And I hope here is a play fitted.

60   **SNUG.** Have you the lion's part written? Pray you, if it be, give it me, for I am slow of study.

   QUINCE. You may do it <u>extempore</u>, for it is nothing but roaring.

   BOTTOM. Let me play the lion too. I will roar, that I will
65   do any man's heart good to hear me. I will roar, that I will make the Duke say, "Let him roar again; let him roar again."

◄ *What other role does Bottom wish to play?*

   QUINCE. And you should do it too terribly, you would fright the Duchess and the ladies, that they would
70   shrike;[11] and that were enough to hang us all.

   ALL. That would hang us, every mother's son.

◄ *What is the group concerned about? What does Bottom claim he can do?*

   BOTTOM. I grant you, friends, if you should fright the ladies out of their wits, they would have no more <u>discretion</u> but to hang us; but I will aggravate[12] my
75   voice so that I will roar you as gently as any sucking dove; I will roar you and 'twere any nightingale.

   QUINCE. You can play no part but Pyramus; for Pyramus is a sweetfac'd man; a proper[13] man as one shall see in a

◄ *According to Quince, why must Bottom take the role of Pyramus?*

---

11. **shrike.** Shriek
12. **aggravate.** Bottom means *moderate* or *calm.*
13. **proper.** Good-looking

Words For Everyday Use	
ex • tem • po • re (eks tem´pə rē) *adv.*, without preparation	
dis • cre • tion (dis kresh´ən) *n.*, power to act or judge; prudence	

summer's day; a most lovely gentlemanlike man:
80 therefore you must needs play Pyramus.

BOTTOM. Well; I will undertake it. What beard were I best to play it in?

QUINCE. Why, what you will.

BOTTOM. I will discharge it in either your strawcolor
85 beard, your orange-tawny beard, your purple-in-grain[14] beard, or your French-crown-color[15] beard, your perfit[16] yellow.

QUINCE. Some of your French crowns have no hair at all;[17] and then you will play barefac'd. But, masters,
90 here are your parts, and I am to entreat you, request you, and desire you, to con[18] them by tomorrow night; and meet me in the palace wood, a mile without the town, by moonlight; there will we rehearse; for if we meet in the city, we shall be dogg'd with company, and
95 our devices known. In the mean time I will draw a bill of properties,[19] such as our play wants. I pray you fail me not.

BOTTOM. We will meet, and there we may rehearse most obscenely[20] and courageously. Take pains, be perfit,
100 adieu.

QUINCE. At the Duke's oak we meet.

BOTTOM. Enough; hold, or cut bow-strings.[21]   *Exeunt.*

▶ *Where and when does the group plan to rehearse?*

---

13. **proper.** Good-looking
14. **purple-in-grain.** Dyed purple
15. **French-crown-color.** Gold-colored
16. **perfit.** perfect
17. **French . . . hair.** Quince is playing on Bottom's words to poke fun at one symptom of a disease then called the "French disease," syphilis.
18. **con.** Memorize; learn
19. **bill of properties.** List of props needed for the play
20. **obscenely.** Another of Bottom's verbal blunders
21. **hold . . . bow-strings.** Uncertain expression; the sense is keep your word or the project is finished

Responding to the Selection

Imagine that you are in Theseus's position and that Egeus has come to you to complain about his daughter's refusal to marry the man he has chosen for her. He asks you to uphold Athenian law and have his daughter killed or sent to a convent should she persist in her refusal. Would you uphold Athenian law or break it? Would you choose some other option? Explain. What might you say to Egeus?

Reviewing the Selection

Recalling and Interpreting

1. **R:** What event do Theseus and Hippolyta await?

2. **I:** How do Hippolyta and Theseus seem to feel about this upcoming event? Explain why their past relationship might be considered unusual.

3. **R:** Who comes to Theseus to air a grievance? What does this person want Theseus to do? Why does Hermia disobey her father? What do Lysander and Hermia say to plead their case? Do their pleas work?

4. **I:** In what way does the situation brought before Theseus's attention compare and contrast with Theseus's own personal situation? How would you characterize Egeus as a father? What are your first impressions of Hermia and Lysander? Who is right? Demetrius is aware of the punishment that Hermia will receive if she should disobey Egeus's wishes. Explain then whether Demetrius truly loves Hermia.

5. **R:** What do Lysander and Hermia plan to do? When Helena meets Hermia and Lysander, why is she upset? What relationship once existed between her and Demetrius? What relationship exists between her and Hermia? At the end of act I, scene i, what does Helena decide to do?

6. **I:** Explain whether you think that Lysander's plan is the best possible course of action. Why aren't Hermia and Lysander willing to accept Theseus's decision? In what way is Demetrius's reaction to Hermia and Helena unusual, given the young women's behavior? Why might the relationship that exists between Hermia and Helena make Demetrius's behavior especially painful to Helena? What motivates Helena to betray Hermia and Lysander to Demetrius?

7. **R:** Why are Quince, Snug, Bottom, Flute, Snout, and Starveling meeting? What are they planning to do, and when? List some of the parts that Bottom wishes to play. Where and when does the group of artisans plan to rehearse? Who else is planning to be in this place at that time?

8. **I:** Why is Quince's description of the play as a "comedy" and Bottom's description of the play as "merry" unusual given its subject matter? How do Bottom's companions seem to view him? How does Bottom seem to view his acting abilities? How would you characterize Bottom? How do you think any of the four lovers, Helena, Hermia, Demetrius, or Lysander, would view Bottom if they were to encounter him in the wood?

Synthesizing

9. Reexamine the following dialogue from act I, scene i:

> LYSANDER. Ay me! for aught that I could ever read,
> Could ever hear by tale or history,
> The course of true love never did run smooth;
> But either it was different in blood—
>
> HERMIA. O cross! too high to be enthrall'd to low.
>
> LYSANDER. Or else misgraffed in respect of years—
>
> HERMIA. O spite! too old to be engag'd to young.
>
> LYSANDER. Or else it stood upon the choice of
> friends—
>
> HERMIA. O hell, to choose love by another's eyes!
>
> LYSANDER. Or if there were a sympathy in choice,
> War, death, or sickness did lay siege to it,
> Making it momentany as a sound,
> Swift as a shadow, short as any dream,
> Brief as the lightning in the collied night,
> That, in a spleen, unfolds both heaven and earth;
> And ere a man hath power to say "Behold!"
> The jaws of darkness do devour it up:
> So quick bright things come to confusion.

To what is love compared in these lines? What attitude does the young couple reveal toward love? Explain whether this is the natural result of their experiences. In what sense is such an attitude toward love unnatural given their relationship with one another? Do they seem to think their love will last forever, or do they see it as fleeting? Compare and contrast Lysander and Hermia's relationship with that of Theseus and Hippolyta. Which couple appears to have the more solid relationship? Is one relationship mature and the other immature? What have Theseus and Hippolyta experienced in their relationship that Lysander and Hermia have not? In what way might experience or "growing up" change Lysander's and Hermia's view of love?

10. Relationships between parents and children were more formal in Shakespeare's time than in our own. Children owed obedience and respect to their parents at all times, even in matters of choosing an occupation or spouse. Thus, Egeus's behavior probably seemed less stern and tyrannical to Shakespeare's audience and Hermia's refusal to obey her father probably seemed far more brash and impertinent. Still, even in Shakespeare's day, Egeus would probably have seemed a little extreme in his attitude toward his daughter. Why do you think he is so extreme? How do you think Shakespeare viewed Egeus? Theseus claims that he is unable to extenuate or lessen the severity of the law and so supports Egeus's position. Explain whether you think Theseus was truly forced to follow the letter of the law or whether you think he could excuse Hermia from such harsh punishment if he truly wished. How would you describe Theseus as a ruler?

Understanding Literature (QUESTIONS FOR DISCUSSION)

1. Inciting Incident and Central Conflict. The **inciting incident** is the event that introduces the central conflict. A **central conflict** is the primary struggle in the plot of a story or drama. What event or action in act I would you describe as the inciting incident? What do you believe will be the central conflict in this drama?

2. Scene and Mood. A **scene** is a short section of a literary work that presents action that occurs in a single place or at a single time. **Mood,** or **atmosphere,** is the emotion created in the reader by part or all of a literary work. Act I of A Midsummer Night's Dream is divided into two scenes. In what way does the subject matter and mood of these two scenes differ? How would you characterize each scene? Why do you think Shakespeare chose to juxtapose two such contrasting scenes in the first act?

3. Character, Style, Iambic Pentameter, and Prose. A **character** is a person (or sometimes an animal) who figures in the action of a literary work. **Style** is the manner in which something is said or written. Traditionally, critics and scholars have referred to three levels of style: high style, for formal occasions or lofty subjects; middle style, for ordinary occasions and subjects; and low style, for extremely informal occasions or subjects. In what way do the social classes of the characters presented in act I, scene i, and act I, scene ii, differ? In what style would you say these different groups of characters speak? An **iamb** is a poetic foot containing one weakly stressed syllable followed by one strongly stressed syllable. **Pentameter** is a term for a five-foot line. **Prose** is the broad term used to describe all writing that is not poetry. As a general rule, Shakespeare usually wrote the lines spoken by his characters of noble background or high status in iambic pentameter while he wrote the lines of characters of lower status in prose. The effect is that the characters of high status speak in beautiful, highly elevated language, while the characters of lower status speak in the more common language of everyday life. Compare and contrast the language that characters use in act I, scene i, and the language characters use in act I, scene ii. Which characters speak in poetry—iambic pentameter—and which speak in prose? What other similarities and differences do you note in the speech of these two groups of characters?

4. **Soliloquy.** A **soliloquy** is a speech delivered by a lone character that reveals the speaker's thoughts and feelings. Which of Helena's speeches in act I, scene i, is a soliloquy? What does this soliloquy reveal about Helena? What thoughts and feelings does she express?

Act II

SCENE i: A wood near Athens.

Enter a FAIRY *at one door and* ROBIN GOODFELLOW (PUCK) *at another.*

PUCK. How now, spirit, whither wander you?

FAIRY. Over hill, over <u>dale</u>,
    Thorough[1] bush, thorough brier,
    Over park, over pale,[2]
5   Thorough flood, thorough fire,
    I do wander every where,
    Swifter than the moon's sphere;
    And I serve the Fairy Queen,
    To dew her orbs[3] upon the green.
10   The cowslips tall her pensioners[4] be:
    In their gold coats spots you see;
    Those be rubies, fairy favors,
    In those freckles live their savors.[5]
    I must go seek some dewdrops here,
15   And hang a pearl in every cowslip's ear.
    Farewell, thou lob[6] of spirits; I'll be gone.
    Our Queen and all her elves come here anon.[7]

PUCK. The King doth keep his revels here tonight;
    Take heed the Queen come not within his sight;
20   For Oberon is passing fell and wrath,[8]
    Because that she as her attendant hath
    A lovely boy stolen from an Indian king;
    She never had so sweet a changeling.[9]
    And jealous Oberon would have the child

◀ *Why does Puck warn the fairy not to let the Fairy Queen encounter the Fairy King?*

◀ *What is the source of the disagreement between the king and queen?*

ACT II, SCENE i
  1. **Thorough.** Through
  2. **pale.** Territory enclosed within bounds
  3. **orbs.** Fairy rings
  4. **pensioners.** Queen Elizabeth I's noble bodyguards were called pensioners
  5. **savors.** Perfumes
  6. **lob.** Big, slow, clumsy person
  7. **anon.** Soon
  8. **passing fell and wrath.** Very fierce or terrible and angry
  9. **changeling.** Usually refers to a child a fairy leaves in place of a human child the fairy steals away; here, refers to the human child the queen of the fairies has stolen

Words For Everyday Use   **dale** (dāl) *n.*, valley

25   Knight of his train, to trace[10] the forests wild;
But she, perforce,[11] withholds the loved boy,
Crowns him with flowers, and makes him all her joy.
And now they never meet in grove or green,
By fountain clear, or <u>spangled</u> starlight sheen,
30   But they do square,[12] that all their elves for fear
Creep into acorn cups, and hide them there.

FAIRY.   Either I mistake your shape and making quite,
Or else you are that shrewd and <u>knavish</u> sprite

► What is Puck's reputation? What mischievous deeds has he been known to do? What kind deeds?

Call'd Robin Goodfellow. Are not you he
35   That frights the maidens of the villagery,
Skim milk, and sometimes labor in the quern,[13]
And bootless[14] make the breathless huswife[15] churn,
And sometime make the drink to bear no barm,[16]
Mislead night-wanderers, laughing at their harm?
40   Those that Hobgoblin call you, and sweet Puck,
You do their work, and they shall have good luck.
Are not you he?

PUCK.   Thou speakest aright;
I am that merry wanderer of the night.
I jest to Oberon and make him smile
45   When I a fat and beanfed horse beguile,
Neighing in likeness of a filly foal;
And sometime lurk I in a gossip's[17] bowl,
In very likeness of a roasted crab,[18]
And when she drinks, against her lips I bob,
50   And on her withered dewlop[19] pour the ale.

► How does Puck feel about his pranks?

The wisest aunt, telling the saddest tale,
Sometime for three-foot stool mistaketh me;
Then slip I from her bum, down topples she,
And "tailor"[20] cries, and falls into a cough;

---

10. **trace.** Traverse; cross
11. **perforce.** By force
12. **square.** Argue
13. **quern.** Hand mill for grinding grain
14. **bootless.** Fruitlessly
15. **huswife.** Housewife
16. **barm.** Yeast; this line may mean Puck prevents the drink from fermenting.
17. **gossip's.** Belonging to an old talkative woman
18. **crab.** Crab apple
19. **dewlop.** Loose fold of skin hanging beneath the chin
20. **tailor.** Refers to the way tailors used to sew, cross-legged on the floor

Words
For
Everyday
Use

span • gled (spaṇ´gəld) *adj.,* decorated with small bright objects that glitter
knav • ish (nāv´ish) *adj.,* dishonest; roguish; tricky

55   And then the whole quire[21] hold their hips and loff,
        And <u>waxen</u> in their mirth, and neeze,[22] and swear
        A merrier hour was never wasted[23] there.
        But room, fairy! here comes Oberon.

        FAIRY. And here my mistress. Would that he were gone!

Enter the King of Fairies (OBERON) at one door with his
TRAIN, and the Queen (TITANIA) at another with hers.

60   **OBERON.** Ill met by moonlight, proud Titania.

        TITANIA. What, jealous Oberon? Fairies, skip hence—
        I have forsworn his bed and company.

        OBERON. Tarry, <u>rash</u> wanton![24] Am not I thy lord?

        TITANIA. Then I must be thy lady; but I know
65   When thou hast stolen away from fairy land,
        And in the shape of Corin sat all day,
        Playing on pipes of corn, and versing love,
        To amorous Phillida.[25] Why art thou here
        Come from the farthest steep[26] of India?
70   But that, forsooth,[27] the bouncing Amazon,
        Your buskin'd[28] mistress, and your warrior love,
        To Theseus must be wedded, and you come
        To give their bed joy and prosperity.

        OBERON. How canst thou thus for shame, Titania,
75   Glance at my credit with Hippolyta,[29]
        Knowing I know thy love to Theseus?
        Didst not thou lead him through the glimmering night
        From Perigenia, whom he ravished?
        And make him with fair Aegles break his faith,
80   With Ariadne, and Antiopa?[30]

◄ *Of what do the*
queen and the king
accuse each other?

---

21. **quire.** Company; group
22. **neeze.** Sneeze
23. **wasted.** Spent
24. **wanton.** Capricious, unrestrained person
25. **Corin . . . Phillida.** Corin and Phillida are conventional names in pastoral
poetry; Titania is accusing her husband of putting on the appearance of a simple
rustic man to play an instrument of grain stalks and flirt with a country girl.
26. **steep.** Mountain
27. **forsooth.** In truth; no doubt
28. **buskin'd.** Wearing hunting boots that reach to the calf
29. **Glance . . . Hippolyta.** Tarnish my reputation by accusing me of loving
Hippolyta
30. **Perigenia . . . Antiopa.** Perigenia, Aegles, Ariadne, and Antiopa were all
women Theseus loved and deserted in classical myths and tales.

Words For Everyday Use	**wax** (waks) *vi.,* increase in strength, intensity, volume (*waxen* is an archaic plural form of the verb; the modern form is *wax*)
	rash (rash) *adj.,* too hasty in acting or speaking

► What has Titania and Oberon's argument caused? How have the floods caused by the "contagious fogs" affected farmers?

► According to Titania, what has happened to the seasons? Why has this happened?

TITANIA. These are the forgeries of jealousy;
And never, since the middle summer's spring,[31]
Met we on hill, in dale, forest, or mead,
By paved[32] fountain or by rushy brook,
85 Or in the beached margent[33] of the sea,
To dance our ringlets[34] to the whistling wind,
But with thy brawls thou hast disturb'd our sport.
Therefore the winds, piping to us in vain,
As in revenge, have suck'd up from the sea
90 Contagious[35] fogs; which, falling in the land,
Hath every pelting[36] river made so proud
That they have overborne their continents.[37]
The ox hath therefore stretch'd his yoke in vain,
The ploughman lost his sweat, and the green corn
95 Hath rotted ere his youth attain'd a beard.[38]
The fold stands empty in the drowned field,
And crows are fatted with the murrion flock;[39]
The nine men's morris[40] is fill'd up with mud,
And the quaint mazes in the wanton green,[41]
100 For lack of tread, are undistinguishable.
The human mortals want their winter here;
No night is now with hymn or carol blest.
Therefore the moon (the governess of floods),
Pale in her anger, washes all the air,
105 That rheumatic diseases[42] do abound.
And thorough this distemperature,[43] we see
The seasons alter: hoary-headed frosts
Fall in the fresh lap of the crimson rose,
And on old Hiems'[44] thin and icy crown
110 An odorous chaplet[45] of sweet summer buds
Is, as in mockery, set; the spring, the summer,
The childing[46] autumn, angry winter, change

---

31. **middle summer's spring.** Beginning of midsummer
32. **paved.** With a pebbly bottom
33. **margent.** Shore
34. **ringlets.** Dance in a little ring or circle
35. **Contagious.** Carrying disease or pestilence
36. **pelting.** Paltry
37. **continents.** Banks
38. **beard.** Referring to the tassel on a ripe ear of corn
39. **murrion flock.** Sheep and cows dead of murrain, an infectious cattle disease
40. **nine men's morris.** Area of land where a game by the same name is played
41. **quaint mazes in the wanton green.** Intricate paths through wild-growing grass (children ran through these paths rapidly as a game)
42. **rheumatic diseases.** Various diseases of the connective tissue, such as gout, arthritis, and rheumatic fever
43. **distemperature.** Disturbance in the natural order
44. **Hiems'.** Winter's
45. **odorous chaplet.** Fragrant crown
46. **childing.** Fruitful, abundant

Their wonted liveries;[47] and the mazed[48] world,
By their increase, now knows not which is which.
115 And this same <u>progeny</u> of evils comes
From our debate, from our <u>dissension</u>;
We are their parents and original.

OBERON. Do you amend it then; it lies in you.
Why should Titania cross her Oberon?
120 I do but beg a little changeling boy,
To be my henchman.[49]

TITANIA.   Set your heart at rest;
The fairy land buys not the child of me.
His mother was a vot'ress[50] of my order,
And in the spiced Indian air, by night,
125 Full often hath she gossip'd by my side,
And sat with me on Neptune's[51] yellow sands,
Marking th' embarked traders on the flood;[52]
When we have laugh'd to see the sails conceive
And grow big-bellied with the wanton wind;
130 Which she, with pretty and with swimming <u>gait</u>,
Following (her womb then rich with my young squire)
Would imitate, and sail upon the land
To fetch me trifles, and return again,
As from a voyage, rich with merchandise.
135 But she, being mortal, of that boy did die,[53]
And for her sake do I rear up her boy;
And for her sake I will not part with him.

OBERON. How long within this wood intend you stay?

TITANIA. Perchance till after Theseus' wedding-day.
140 If you will patiently dance in our round,[54]
And see our moonlight revels, go with us;
If not, <u>shun</u> me, and I will spare[55] your haunts.

OBERON. Give me that boy, and I will go with thee.

◄ Why won't
Titania part with the
child Oberon wishes
to make his page? To
what does she com-
pare the child's
mother?

---

47. **wonted liveries.** Usual apparel
48. **mazed.** Amazed; bewildered
49. **henchman.** Page
50. **vot'ress.** Woman bound by a vow or promise; devoted or ardent supporter
51. **Neptune's.** Belonging to Neptune, Roman god of the sea
52. **Marking . . . flood.** Watching the trade ships on the water
53. **of . . . die.** Died giving birth to the child
54. **round.** Dance in which the dancers move in a circle or ring
55. **spare.** Avoid; stay away from

Words For Everyday Use	
prog • e • ny (präj´ə nē) *n.*, descendants or offspring
dis • sen • sion (di sen´shen) *n.*, difference of opinion
gait (gāt) *n.*, manner of moving on foot
shun (shun) *vt.*, keep away from

TITANIA. Not for thy fairy kingdom. Fairies, away!
145 We shall chide downright, if I longer stay.

Exeunt TITANIA *and her* TRAIN.

▶ What promise
does Oberon make?

OBERON. Well; go thy way. Thou shalt not from[56] this grove
Till I torment thee for this injury.[57]
My gentle Puck, come hither. Thou rememb'rest
Since once I sat upon a <u>promontory</u>,
150 And heard a mermaid on a dolphin's back
Uttering such <u>dulcet</u> and harmonious breath
That the rude sea grew civil[58] at her song,
And certain stars shot madly from their spheres,
To hear the sea-maid's music?

PUCK.   I remember.

▶ What did Cupid
try to do?

155 **OBERON.** That very time I saw (but thou couldst not),
Flying between the cold moon and the earth,
Cupid all arm'd. A certain aim he took
At a fair vestal[59] throned by the west,
And loos'd his love-shaft smartly from his bow,
160 As it should pierce a hundred thousand hearts;
But I might see young Cupid's fiery shaft
Quench'd in the chaste beams of the wat'ry moon,
And the imperial vot'ress passed on,
In maiden meditation, fancy-free.[60]

▶ What happened
to transform the
flower? What unusual
power does the juice
of this flower have?

165 Yet mark'd I where the bolt of Cupid fell.
It fell upon a little western flower,
Before milk-white, now purple with love's wound,
And maidens call it love-in-idleness.[61]
Fetch me that flow'r; the herb I showed thee once.
170 The juice of it on sleeping eyelids laid
Will make or man or woman madly dote
Upon the next live creature that it sees.
Fetch me this herb, and be thou here again
Ere the leviathan[62] can swim a league.

---

56. **from.** Leave; depart
57. **injury.** Offense against a person's feelings or dignity
58. **rude . . . civil.** Rough sea grew calm or placid; with a play on impolite and polite behavior
59. **vestal.** Virgin; a compliment to Queen Elizabeth, also called the Virgin Queen
60. **fancy-free.** Free of love
61. **love-in-idleness.** Nickname for the pansy
62. **leviathan.** Large sea creature; whale

Words For Everyday Use	**prom • on • to • ry** (präm´ən tôr´ē) *n.,* peak of high land that juts out into a body of water **dul • cet** (dul´sit) *adj.,* soothing or pleasant to hear; sweet-sounding

175   PUCK. I'll put a girdle round about the earth
     In forty minutes.   *Exit.*

     OBERON.   Having once this juice,
     I'll watch Titania when she is asleep,
     And drop the liquor of it in her eyes;
     The next thing then she waking looks upon
180   (Be it on lion, bear, or wolf, or bull,
     On meddling monkey, or on busy ape),
     She shall pursue it with the soul of love.
     And ere I take this charm from off her sight
     (As I can take it with another herb),
185   I'll make her render up her page to me.
     But who comes here? I am invisible,
     And I will overhear their conference.

     Enter DEMETRIUS, HELENA *following him.*

     DEMETRIUS. I love thee not; therefore pursue me not.
     Where is Lysander and fair Hermia?
190   The one I'll slay; the other slayeth me.
     Thou toldst me they were stol'n unto this wood;
     And here am I, and wode[63] within this wood,
     Because I cannot meet my Hermia.
     Hence, get thee gone, and follow me no more.

195   HELENA. You draw me, you hardhearted adamant;[64]
     But yet you draw not iron, for my heart
     Is true as steel: Leave you your power to draw,
     And I shall have no power to follow you.

     DEMETRIUS. Do I entice you? Do I speak you fair?[65]
200   Or rather do I not in plainest truth
     Tell you I do not nor I cannot love you?

     HELENA. And even for that do I love you the more.
     I am your spaniel; and, Demetrius,
     The more you beat me, I will fawn on you.
205   Use me but as your spaniel; spurn me, strike me,
     Neglect me, lose me; only give me leave,
     Unworthy as I am, to follow you.
     What worser place can I beg in your love

◄ What does Oberon plan to do to acquire the changeling boy from Titania?

◄ How does Demetrius feel about Helena following him? How does he feel about Lysander? about Hermia?

◄ What does Helena say she will continue to do regardless of Demetrius's cruel actions? How would you describe her speech?

---

63. **wode.** Insane
64. **adamant.** Hard stone that was believed to be unbreakable; magnet
65. **speak you fair.** Speak to you kindly and politely

Words For Everyday Use

en • tice (en tīs´) *vt.,* attract by offering hope or reward of pleasure

spurn (spurn) *vt.,* push or drive away contemptuously or scornfully

(And yet a place of high respect with me)
210 Than to be used as you use your dog?

DEMETRIUS. Tempt not too much the hatred of my spirit,
For I am sick when I do look on thee.

HELENA. And I am sick when I look not on you.

DEMETRIUS. You do impeach[66] your modesty too much,
215 To leave the city and commit yourself
Into the hands of one that loves you not;
To trust the opportunity of night,
And the ill counsel of a desert[67] place,
With the rich worth of your virginity.

220 HELENA. Your virtue is my privilege.[68] For that
It is not night when I do see your face,
Therefore I think I am not in the night,
Nor doth this wood lack worlds of company,
For you in my respect[69] are all the world.
225 Then how can it be said I am alone,
When all the world is here to look on me?

DEMETRIUS. I'll run from thee, and hide me in the
brakes,[70]
And leave thee to the mercy of wild beasts.

HELENA. The wildest hath not such a heart as you.
230 Run when you will; the story shall be chang'd:
Apollo flies, and Daphne holds the chase;[71]
The dove pursues the griffin;[72] the mild hind[73]
Makes speed to catch the tiger—bootless speed,
When cowardice pursues and <u>valor</u> flies.

235 DEMETRIUS. I will not stay[74] thy questions. Let me go;
Or if thou follow me, do not believe
But I shall do thee mischief in the wood.

<blockquote>
► According to Demetrius, why is Helena's decision to follow him unwise?
</blockquote>

<blockquote>
► What does Demetrius threaten to do?
</blockquote>

---

66. **impeach.** Call into question
67. **desert.** Deserted
68. **Your . . . privilege.** Your noble nature is my license for doing so.
69. **respect.** Opinion; estimation
70. **brakes.** Thickets; briers
71. **the story . . . chase.** In the original story Apollo, maddened by love, chases the unwilling nymph Daphne, whose prayers are answered when she is changed into a laurel tree to escape Apollo's advances; Helena is pointing out that this situation is reversed and that she is the pursuer.
72. **griffin.** Legendary monster with the head of an eagle and the body of a lion
73. **hind.** Female deer
74. **stay.** Stay to listen to

Words For Everyday Use

val • or (val′ər) *n.*, courage or bravery

HELENA. Ay, in the temple, in the town, the field,
You do me mischief. Fie, Demetrius!
240   Your wrongs do set a scandal on my sex.[75]
We cannot fight for love, as men may do.
We should be woo'd, and were not made to woo.

Exit DEMETRIUS.

I'll follow thee and make a heaven of hell
To die upon[76] the hand I love so well.   *Exit.*

245   OBERON. Fare thee well, nymph. Ere he do leave this grove,
Thou shalt fly him, and he shall seek thy love.

Enter PUCK.

Hast thou the flower there? Welcome, wanderer.

PUCK. Ay, there it is.

OBERON.   I pray thee give it me.
I know a bank where the wild thyme blows[77]
250   Where oxlips and the nodding violet grows,
Quite over-canopied with luscious woodbine,
With sweet musk-roses and with eglantine;[78]
There sleeps Titania sometime of the night
Lull'd in these flowers with dances and delight;
255   And there the snake throws[79] her enamell'd skin,
Weed[80] wide enough to wrap a fairy in;
And with the juice of this I'll streak her eyes,
And make her full of hateful fantasies.
Take thou some of it, and seek through this grove;
260   A sweet Athenian lady is in love
With a disdainful youth; anoint his eyes,
But do it when the next thing he espies
May be the lady. Thou shalt know the man
By the Athenian garments he hath on.
265   Effect it with some care, that he may prove
More fond on her[81] than she upon her love;
And look thou meet me ere the first cock crow.

PUCK. Fear not, my lord! your servant shall do so.

Exeunt.

◄ What does
Oberon vow? How
does he seem to feel
about the scene he
has just witnessed?

◄ What does
Oberon order Puck to
do while he carries
out his plan upon
Titania?

---

75. **Your . . . sex.** Your deeds cause me to behave in a manner that is scandalous
for a woman.
76. **upon.** By
77. **blows.** Blooms
78. **oxlips . . . eglantine.** *Oxlips*—yellow flower that blooms in early spring; *woodbine*—type of honeysuckle with fragrant yellow-white blossoms; *musk-roses*—fragrant
rose usually with white flowers; *eglantine*—variety of rose usually with pink flowers
79. **throws.** Sheds
80. **Weed.** Garment
81. **fond on her.** Foolishly in love with her

SCENE ii: The wood.

Enter TITANIA, *Queen of Fairies, with her* TRAIN.

▶ How large are the fairies supposed to be? How can you tell?

bats / evles

TITANIA. Come, now a roundel[1] and a fairy song;
Then, for the third part of a minute, hence,
Some to kill cankers[2] in the muskrose buds,
Some war with rere-mice[3] for their leathren wings
5   To make my small elves coats, and some keep back
The clamorous owl, that nightly hoots and wonders
At our quaint[4] spirits. Sing me now asleep;
Then to your offices, and let me rest.

FAIRIES *sing.*

FIRST FAIRY. You spotted snakes with double tongue,
10   Thorny hedgehogs, be not seen,
        Newts and blind-worms, do no wrong,
        Come not near our fairy queen.

CHORUS. Philomele,[5] with melody,
        Sing in our sweet lullaby,
15   Lulla, lulla, lullaby, lulla, lulla, lullaby.
        Never harm,
        Nor spell, nor charm,
        Come our lovely lady nigh.
        So good night, with lullaby.

20   FIRST FAIRY. Weaving spiders, come not here;
        Hence, you longlegg'd spinners, hence!
        Beetles black, approach not near;
        Worm nor snail, do no offense.

CHORUS.   Philomele, with melody, etc.

25   SECOND FAIRY. Hence, away! now all is well.
        One aloof stand sentinel.

Exeunt FAIRIES. TITANIA *sleeps.*

Enter OBERON *and squeezes the flower on* TITANIA'S *eyelids.*

▶ What does Oberon hope that Titania will do?

OBERON. What thou seest when thou dost wake,
        Do it for thy true-love take;
        Love and languish for his sake.
30   Be it ounce,[6] or cat, or bear,
        Pard,[7] or boar with bristled hair,
        In thy eye that shall appear

ACT II, SCENE ii
1. **roundel.** Dance in which the dancers move in a circle or ring
2. **cankers.** Worms
3. **rere-mice.** Bats
4. **quaint.** Unusually dainty
5. **Philomele.** Poetic term for a nightingale
6. **ounce.** Lynx, snow leopard
7. **Pard.** Leopard

When thou wak'st, it is thy dear:
Wake when some <u>vile</u> thing is near.   *Exit.*

Enter LYSANDER *and* HERMIA.

35 LYSANDER. Fair love, you faint with wand'ring in the
   wood
   And to speak troth[8] I have forgot our way.
   We'll rest us, Hermia, if you think it good,
   And <u>tarry</u> for the comfort of the day.

   HERMIA. Be't so, Lysander. Find you out a bed;
40 For I upon this bank will rest my head.

   LYSANDER. One turf shall serve as pillow for us both,
   One heart, one bed, two bosoms, and one troth.[9]

   HERMIA. Nay, good Lysander; for my sake, my dear,
   Lie further off yet; do not lie so near.

45 LYSANDER. O, take the sense, sweet, of my innocence!
   Love takes the meaning in love's conference:[10]
   I mean, that my heart unto yours is knit,
   So that but one heart we can make of it;
   Two bosoms interchained with an oath,
50 So then two bosoms and a single troth.
   Then by your side no bed-room me deny
   For lying so, Hermia, I do not lie.

   HERMIA. Lysander riddles very prettily.
   Now much beshrew[11] my manners and my pride,
55 If Hermia meant to say Lysander lied.
   But, gentle friend, for love and courtesy,
   Lie further off, in humane modesty;
   Such separation as may well be said
   Becomes a virtuous bachelor and a maid,
60 So far be distant; and good night, sweet friend.
   Thy love ne'er alter till thy sweet life end!

   LYSANDER. Amen, amen, to that fair prayer, say I,
   And then end life when I end loyalty!
   Here is my bed; sleep give thee all his rest!

◄ What does
Hermia insist on?

Sleeping
w/ lysander

---

8. **troth.** Truth
9. **troth.** Pledge to marry
10. **Love . . . conference.** Lovers should be able to understand what one
another mean
11. **beshrew.** Mild curse

Words For Everyday Use

vile (vīl) *adj.,* repulsive; disgusting
tar • ry (tar´ē) *vi.,* stay for a time; remain temporarily

65   HERMIA. With half that wish the wisher's eyes be press'd![12]

                                           They sleep.

Enter PUCK.

   PUCK. Through the forest have I gone,
        But Athenian found I none,
        On whose eyes I might approve[13]
        This flower's force in stirring love.
70   Night and silence—Who is here?
        Weeds[14] of Athens he doth wear:
        This is he, my master said,
        Despised the Athenian maid;
        And here the maiden, sleeping sound,
75   On the <u>dank</u> and dirty ground.
        Pretty soul, she durst not lie
        Near this lack-love, this kill-courtesy.
        Churl,[15] upon thy eyes I throw
        All the power this charm doth owe.[16]
80   When thou wak'st, let love forbid
        Sleep his seat on thy eyelid.
        So awake when I am gone,
        For I must now to Oberon.   *Exit.*

Enter DEMETRIUS *and* HELENA, *running.*

   HELENA. Stay—though thou kill me, sweet Demetrius.

85   DEMETRIUS. I charge thee hence, and do not haunt me
      thus.

   HELENA. O, wilt thou darkling[17] leave me? do not so.

   DEMETRIUS. Stay, on thy peril; I alone will go.   *Exit.*

   HELENA. O, I am out of breath in this fond chase!
        The more my prayer, the lesser is my grace.
90   Happy is Hermia, wheresoe'er she lies,
        For she hath blessed and attractive eyes.
        How came her eyes so bright? Not with salt tears;
        If so, my eyes are oft'ner wash'd than hers.

► *Whom does Puck mistake for the "disdainful youth" that Oberon intended him to find? Why does Puck make this mistake?*

► *What does Demetrius do to Helena?*

he left her alone in the dark

---

12. **With . . . press'd.** Lysander wished Hermia "all" sleep's rest, so Hermia wishes Lysander a half of sleep's rest so that he too will sleep well.
13. **approve.** Prove by testing
14. **Weeds.** Clothes, garments
15. **Churl.** Surly, ill-bred person
16. **owe.** Own, possess
17. **darkling.** In the dark

Words For Everyday Use   **dank** (daŋk) *adj.,* disagreeably damp; moist and chilly

No, no; I am as ugly as a bear;
95 For beasts that meet me run away for fear.
Therefore no marvel though Demetrius
Do, as a monster, fly my presence thus.
What wicked and <u>dissembling</u> glass[18] of mine
Made me compare with Hermia's sphery eyne![19]
100 But who is here? Lysander! on the ground?
Dead, or asleep? I see no blood, no wound.
Lysander, if you live, good sir, awake.

LYSANDER. [*Awaking.*] And run through fire I will for thy
    sweet sake.
Transparent[20] Helena, nature shows art,
105 That through thy bosom makes me see thy heart.
Where is Demetrius? O, how fit a word
Is that vile name to perish on my sword!

HELENA. Do not say so, Lysander, say not so.
What though he love your Hermia? Lord, what though?
110 Yet Hermia still loves you; then be content.

LYSANDER. Content with Hermia? No; I do repent
The tedious minutes I with her have spent.
<u>Not Hermia, but Helena I love.</u>
<u>Who will not change a raven for a dove?</u>
115 The will of man is by his reason sway'd;
And reason says you are the worthier maid.
Things growing are not ripe until their season,
So I, being young, till now ripe not to reason;
And touching now the point of human skill,[21]
120 Reason becomes the marshal to my will,[22]
And leads me to your eyes, where I o'erlook
Love's stories written in Love's richest book.

HELENA. Wherefore was I to this keen mockery born?
When at your hands did I deserve this scorn?
125 Is't not enough, is't not enough, young man,
That I did never, no, nor never can,
Deserve a sweet look from Demetrius' eye

◄ What happens
when Helena wakes
Lysander?

*he hits
on her.*

◄ How does
Lysander feel about
Hermia now?

*He swoned
on her*

◄ In what way does
Helena interpret
Lysander's declara-
tion of love for her?

*as an
Insult*

---

18. **glass.** Mirror
19. **sphery eyne.** Eyes as bright as the stars
20. **Transparent.** Bright; capable of being seen through
21. **And . . . skill.** And now being fully reasonable
22. **Reason . . . will.** Reason leads my desire

But you must flout my <u>insufficiency</u>?
Good troth, you do me wrong (good sooth,[23] you do)
130 In such disdainful manner me to woo.
But fare you well; perforce I must confess
I thought you lord of more true gentleness.[24]
O that a lady, of one man refus'd
Should of another therefore be abus'd!   *Exit.*

▶ What does
Lysander do to
Hermia?

[handwritten: wants to swerve]

135 LYSANDER. She sees not Hermia. Hermia, sleep thou
          there,
And never mayst thou come Lysander near!
For as a <u>surfeit</u> of the sweetest things
The deepest loathing to the stomach brings,
Or as the heresies that men do leave
140 Are hated most of those they did deceive,[25]
So thou, my surfeit and my heresy,
Of all be hated, but the most of me!
And, all my powers, address your love and might
To honor Helen and to be her knight.   *Exit.*

▶ What has Hermia
dreamed?

[handwritten: Ly sat and smiled as she was eaten]

145 HERMIA. [*Starting up.*] Help me, Lysander, help me! do
          thy best
To pluck this crawling serpent from my breast!
Ay me, for pity! what a dream was here!
Lysander, look how I do quake with fear.
Methought a serpent eat my heart away,
150 And you sate[26] smiling at his cruel prey.[27]
Lysander! what, remov'd? Lysander! lord!
What, out of hearing gone? No sound, no word?
Alack, where are you? Speak, and if you hear;
Speak, of all loves! I swoon almost with fear.
155 No? then I well perceive you are not nigh:
Either death, or you, I'll find immediately.   *Exit.*

---

23. **Good troth . . . good sooth.** Both phrases mean "in truth; indeed"
24. **gentleness.** Chivalry; good manners and character
25. **heresies . . . deceive.** Foolish beliefs people abandon are hated most by
those who once believed them.
26. **sate.** Sat
27. **prey.** Act of preying upon me

Words
For
Everyday
Use

in • suf • fi • cien • cy (in´sə fish´ən sē) *n.,* inadequacy
sur • feit (sur´fit) *n.,* excess; too great an amount

Responding to the Selection

Imagine that you are Helena's friend and that she comes to you to share her feelings for Demetrius and to tell you about his cruel behavior. She says that she doesn't mind Demetrius using her and spurning her like a dog. What advice would you give her?

Reviewing the Selection

Recalling and Interpreting

1. **R:** What has caused the disagreement between Oberon and Titania? Why won't Titania do what Oberon wishes?

2. **I:** What effect has this disagreement had on the natural world? What do these effects reveal about the fairies' power? about their role in maintaining order in the natural world?

3. **R:** What does Oberon plan to do to obtain what he desires from Titania?

4. **I:** What do you think of Oberon's method of obtaining what he wants? Is his plan fair to his wife, Titania?

5. **R:** After Oberon observes the way Demetrius treats Helena, what does he order Puck to do? What blunder does Puck make in carrying out Oberon's orders?

6. **I:** How would you characterize Demetrius's behavior toward Helena? What has unrequited love done to Helena's sense of self-worth? How can you tell that she feels this way? What motivates Oberon to interfere in human love affairs? Explain why Puck makes this blunder.

7. **R:** Why isn't Hermia the first person Lysander sees when he awakes? What is the result of Puck's blunder? How does Helena interpret Lysander's words? What does Hermia wake to discover? What has she dreamed?

8. **I:** Why does Helena interpret Lysander's words as she does? After Lysander is anointed with the juice of the flower, how would you compare and contrast his behavior to that of Demetrius? In what way is Hermia's dream like her reality? How do you think she feels to wake in this situation?

Synthesizing

9. Based on the behavior of Puck, Titania, and Oberon, what is your view of the fairies? In what ways are they different from humans? In what ways are they similar? Explain whether it is right for them to meddle in human affairs. Do their intentions make up for the result of their actions?

10. In what ways have the four young lovers changed roles or taken on aspects of each other's identities by the end of act II? In what way is Lysander more like Demetrius? In what way have Hermia and Helena become more alike? Explain whether, thus far, Shakespeare has presented love

as static or as fickle and changeable. Why might this be so? What is Shakespeare indicating about the four young lovers?

Understanding Literature (QUESTIONS FOR DISCUSSION)

1. Comedy and Setting. Originally a literary work with a happy ending, a **comedy** is any lighthearted or humorous work, especially one prepared for the stage or screen. The typical progression of the action in a comedy is from initial order to a humorous misunderstanding and back to order again. The **setting** of a literary work is the time and place in which it occurs, together with all the details used to create a sense of a particular time and place. Many of Shakespeare's comedies feature a place of magical wildness to which the main characters retreat from the everyday world. In this place of wildness, the typical rules of everyday conduct change; characters may take on disguises; the identities or perceptions of characters may change as well, either permanently or temporarily; and after some confusion or role reversal, a conflict or misunderstanding is resolved. What is magical, wild, or otherworldy about the wood outside Athens? What humorous misunderstanding or departure from order takes place there? What changes in the behavior of the four young people seem to have occurred in this setting? In what ways have the rules of everyday conduct been altered?

2. Suspension of Disbelief. Suspension of disbelief is the phrase used by poet and critic Samuel Taylor Coleridge in his *Biographia Literaria* to describe the audience's compliance in setting aside skepticism to participate imaginatively in the world of the author's creation. Why might an audience have to suspend disbelief to participate imaginatively in *A Midsummer Night's Dream*? List some examples of events that occur in this act which you might not normally believe. For example, how big are the fairies supposed to be? What evidence of magic do you see? What does Oberon say to explain why he can observe Demetrius and Lysander without himself being observed?

3. Allusion. An **allusion** is a rhetorical technique in which reference is made to a person, event, object, or work from history or literature. Queen Elizabeth was a shrewd leader who remained unmarried, playing the other European states off against each other, as each hoped for an alliance through marriage to the English throne. She was celebrated by her subjects as the "Virgin Queen." In act II, scene i, lines 157–164, Shakespeare alludes, and pays compliment to, Queen Elizabeth as a "fair vestal." What qualities in Elizabeth is Shakespeare praising? Why might Shakespeare have been especially interested in complimenting the queen given that this play was probably first performed before an aristocratic audience?

Act III

SCENE i: The scene continues.

Enter the Clowns [QUINCE, SNUG, BOTTOM, FLUTE, SNOUT, *and* STARVELING].

BOTTOM. Are we all met?

QUINCE. Pat, pat;[1] and here's a marvail's[2] convenient place for our rehearsal. This green plot shall be our stage, this hawthorn brake our tiring-house,[3] and we
5 will do it in action as we will do it before the Duke.

BOTTOM. Peter Quince!

QUINCE. What sayest thou, bully[4] Bottom?

BOTTOM. There are things in this comedy of Pyramus and Thisby that will never please. First, Pyramus must
10 draw a sword to kill himself; which the ladies cannot <u>abide</u>. How answer you that?

SNOUT. By'r lakin, a parlous[5] fear.

STARVELING. I believe we must leave the killing out, when all is done.

15 BOTTOM. Not a whit! I have a device to make all well. Write me a prologue, and let the prologue seem to say we will do no harm with our swords, and that Pyramus is not kill'd indeed; and for the more better assurance, tell them that I Pyramus am not Pyramus, but Bottom
20 the weaver. This will put them out of fear.

QUINCE. Well; we will have such a prologue, and it shall be written in eight and six.[6]

BOTTOM. No; make it two more; let it be written in eight and eight.

25 SNOUT. Will not the ladies be afeard of the lion?

STARVELING. I fear it, I promise you.

BOTTOM. Masters, you ought to consider with yourselves,

◄ *What is the first potential problem Bottom finds with the intended performance?*

◄ *What is Bottom's solution to this problem?*

◄ *What other problem do the players identify?*

1. **Pat, pat.** Timely; opportunely
2. **marvail's.** Marvelous
3. **tiring-house.** Dressing room
4. **bully.** Companion, comrade
5. **By'r lakin, a parlous.** By our lady (Virgin Mary), a perilous or extreme
6. **eight and six.** Alternate lines of eight and six syllables, used in ballads

Words
For
Everyday
Use

a • bide (ə bīd´) *vi.*, submit to; put up with

to bring in (God shield us!) a lion among ladies, is a
most dreadful thing; for there is not a more fearful wild-
30 fowl than your lion living; and we ought to look to't.

SNOUT. Therefore another prologue must tell he is not a
lion.

BOTTOM. Nay; you must name his name, and half his face
must be seen through the lion's neck, and he himself
35 must speak through, saying thus, or to the same defect:[7]
"Ladies," or "Fair ladies, I would wish you," or "I would
request you," or "I would entreat you, not to fear, not to
tremble: my life for yours. If you think I come hither as a
lion, it were pity of my life. No! I am no such thing; I am
40 a man as other men are"; and there indeed let him name
his name, and tell them plainly he is Snug the joiner.

QUINCE. Well; it shall be so. But there is two hard
things: that is, to bring the moonlight into a chamber;
for you know, Pyramus and Thisby meet by moonlight.

45 SNOUT. Doth the moon shine that night we play our play?

BOTTOM. A calendar, a calendar! Look in the almanac.
Find out moonshine, find out moonshine.

QUINCE. Yes; it doth shine that night.

BOTTOM. Why then may you leave a casement of the
50 great chamber window (where we play) open; and the
moon may shine in at the casement.

QUINCE. Ay; or else one must come in with a bush of
thorns and a lantern,[8] and say he comes to disfigure,[9] or
to present, the person of Moonshine. Then, there is
55 another thing: we must have a wall in the great
chamber; for Pyramus and Thisby (says the story) did
talk through the chink[10] of a wall.

SNOUT. You can never bring in a wall. What say you,
Bottom?

60 BOTTOM. Some man or other must present Wall; and let
him have some plaster, or some loam, or some rough-
cast[11] about him, to signify wall; or let him hold his
fingers thus, and through that cranny shall Pyramus
and Thisby whisper.

▶ How does Bottom think that this problem should be solved? What does this solution reveal about Bottom's conception of the role of illusion in the theater?

▶ Explain whose idea about how to represent moonshine you think is better, Bottom's or Quince's.

▶ How does Bottom believe they can represent a wall?

---

7. **defect.** Bottom means "effect."
8. **bush of thorns and a lantern.** People of rural England said the man in the
moon was placed in the sky for collecting wood on the Sabbath; they saw him as
carrying a bundle of sticks, hence the bush of thorns. The lantern represents
moonlight.
9. **disfigure.** Bottom means "figure" or "portray."
10. **chink.** Narrow opening
11. **rough-cast.** Lime mixed with small stones and used as plaster on outside walls

65 QUINCE. If that may be, then all is well. Come, sit down, every mother's son, and rehearse your parts. Pyramus, you begin. When you have spoken your speech, enter into that brake; and so every one according to his cue.

Enter ROBIN (PUCK), *behind.*

◀ What is Puck's opinion of the group of actors? What does he plan to do?

PUCK. What hempen home-spuns[12] have we <u>swaggering</u> here,
70 So near the cradle of the Fairy Queen?
What, a play toward? I'll be an auditor,[13]
An actor too perhaps, if I see cause.

QUINCE. Speak, Pyramus. Thisby, stand forth.

BOTTOM. "Thisby, the flowers of <u>odious</u> savors sweet"—

75 QUINCE. Odorous, odorous.

BOTTOM. —"odors savors sweet;
So hath thy breath, my dearest Thisby dear.
But hark, a voice! Stay thou but here a while,
And by and by I will to thee appear." *Exit.*

80 PUCK. A stranger Pyramus than e'er played here. *Exit.*

FLUTE. Must I speak now?

QUINCE. Ay, marry, must you; for you must understand he goes but to see a noise that he heard, and is to come again.

85 FLUTE. "Most radiant Pyramus, most lily-white of hue,
Of color like the red rose on triumphant brier,
Most brisky juvenal,[14] and eke[15] most lovely Jew,
As true as truest horse, that yet would never tire,
I'll meet thee, Pyramus, at Ninny's[16] tomb."

90 QUINCE. "Ninus' tomb," man. Why, you must not speak that yet. That you answer to Pyramus. You speak all your part at once, cues and all. Pyramus, enter. Your cue is past; it is "never tire."

◀ What complaint does Quince have about Flute's performance as Thisby?

FLUTE. O—"As true as truest horse, that yet would never tire."

---

12. **hempen home-spuns.** Crude, rustic folk
13. **auditor.** Hearer or listener
14. **brisky juvenal.** Energetic youth
15. **eke.** Also
16. **Ninny's.** Flute means to say Ninus's. Ninus was the legendary founder of Nineveh, the Mesopotamian city where the story of Pyramus and Thisby is set.

Words For Everyday Use

swag • ger (swag´ər) *vi.,* boast, brag, or show off in a loud manner
o • di • ous (ō´dē əs) *adj.,* disgusting; offensive

▶ Why do the actors flee from Bottom? Who do you think altered Bottom's appearance?

Enter PUCK, *and* BOTTOM *with an ass's head.*

95   BOTTOM. "If I were fair, Thisby, I were only thine."

QUINCE. O monstrous! O strange! We are haunted. Pray, masters, fly, masters! Help!

     Exeunt QUINCE, SNUG, FLUTE, SNOUT, *and* STARVELING.

PUCK. I'll follow you, I'll lead you about a round,[17]
Through bog, through bush, through brake, through
    brier:
100 Sometime a horse I'll be, sometime a hound
A hog, a headless bear, sometime a fire,
And neigh, and bark, and grunt, and roar, and burn,
Like horse, hound, hog, bear, fire, at every turn.

     Exit.

BOTTOM. Why do they run away? This is a knavery of
105 them to make me afeard.

Enter SNOUT.

SNOUT. O Bottom, thou art chang'd! What do I see on thee?

BOTTOM. What do you see? You see an ass-head of your own,[18] do you?

     Exit SNOUT.

Enter QUINCE.

110 QUINCE. Bless thee, Bottom, bless thee! Thou art
translated.[19]   *Exit.*

▶ What does Bottom believe his companions are doing?

BOTTOM. I see their knavery. This is to make an ass of me, to fright me, if they could; but I will not stir from this place, do what they can. I will walk up and down
115 here, and I will sing, that they shall hear I am not
afraid.   *Sings.*

    The woosel cock[20] so black of hue,
      With orange-tawny bill,
    The throstle with his note so true,
120   The wren with little quill—[21]

▶ Whom does Bottom's singing awake?

TITANIA. [*Awaking.*] What angel wakes me from my
flow'ry bed?

BOTTOM. [*Sings.*]
    The finch, the sparrow, and the lark,

---

17. **about a round.** Roundabout
18. **ass-head . . . own.** Your own foolish fancy or notion
19. **translated.** Transformed
20. **woosel cock.** Blackbird
21. **quill.** Piping voice

The plain-song cuckoo grey,[22]
　　Whose note full many a man doth mark,
125　　And dares not answer nay—
for indeed, who would set his wit to[23] so foolish a bird?
Who would give a bird the lie, though he cry "cuckoo"
never so?[24]

TITANIA. I pray thee, gentle mortal, sing again.
130　Mine ear is much <u>enamored</u> of thy note;
So is mine eye enthralled to thy shape;
And thy fair virtue's force[25] (perforce) doth move me
On the first view to say, to swear, I love thee.

◄ How does Titania feel about Bottom? Why does she feel this way?

BOTTOM. Methinks, mistress, you should have little
135　reason for that. And yet, to say the truth, reason and
love keep little company together now-a-days. The more
the pity that some honest neighbors will not make
them friends. Nay, I can gleek[26] upon occasion.

◄ What does Bottom point out about Titania's declaration of love?

TITANIA. Thou art as wise as thou art beautiful.

140　BOTTOM. Not so, neither; but if I had wit enough to get
out of this wood, I have enough to serve mine owe[27]
turn.

TITANIA. Out of this wood do not desire to go;
Thou shalt remain here, whether thou wilt or no.
145　I am a spirit of no common rate;[28]
The summer still doth tend upon my state;[29]
And I do love thee; therefore go with me.
I'll give thee fairies to attend on thee;
And they shall fetch thee jewels from the deep,
150　And sing while thou on pressed flowers dost sleep.
And I will purge thy mortal grossness[30] so,

◄ What does Titania tell Bottom he cannot do? What does she promise her attendant fairies will do for Bottom?

---

22. **plain-song cuckoo grey.** Gray cuckoo that sings a simple song; in the following lines, Bottom plays on the similarities between the words *cuckoo* and *cuckold,* or man whose wife has committed adultery. Such jests about cuckoos were common in Shakespeare's day.
23. **set his wit to.** Try to answer
24. **Who would . . . never so.** Who would call a bird a liar—even if the bird does cry "cuckoo" (calling him a cuckold) so frequently?
25. **thy fair virtue's force.** The strength or power of your beauty
26. **gleek.** Joke; jest
27. **owe.** Own
28. **rate.** Class or rank
29. **tend . . . state.** Attend me; wait upon me
30. **mortal grossness.** Human condition of having a body

Words
For
Everyday
Use

en • am • or (en am´ər) *vt.,* fill with love and desire;
charm; captivate (mostly used in the passive as it appears
in the line above)

That thou shalt like an aery spirit go.
Peaseblossom! Cobweb! Moth![31] and Mustardseed!

Enter four Fairies (PEASEBLOSSOM, COBWEB, MOTH, *and* MUSTARDSEED.)

PEASEBLOSSOM. Ready.
COBWEB.   And I.
MOTH.   And I.
MUSTARDSEED.   And I.
ALL.   Where shall we go?

155 TITANIA. Be kind and courteous to this gentleman,
Hop in his walks and <u>gambol</u> in his eyes;
Feed him with apricocks[32] and dewberries,
With purple grapes, green figs, and mulberries;
The honey-bags steal from the humble-bees,[33]
160 And for night-tapers crop their waxen thighs,[34]
And light them at the fiery glow-worm's eyes,
To have my love to bed and to arise;
And pluck the wings from painted butterflies,
To fan the moonbeams from his sleeping eyes.
165 Nod to him, elves, and do him courtesies.

PEASEBLOSSOM. Hail, mortal!

COBWEB. Hail!

MOTH. Hail!

MUSTARDSEED. Hail!

▶ *How would you characterize Bottom's behavior toward the fairies?*

170 BOTTOM. I cry your worship's mercy,[35] heartily. I <u>beseech</u> your worship's name.

COBWEB. Cobweb.

BOTTOM. I shall desire you of more acquaintance,[36] good Master Cobweb. If I cut my finger, I shall make
175 bold with you.[37] Your name, honest gentleman?

---

31. **Moth.** Mote, speck
32. **apricocks.** Apricots
33. **humble-bees.** Bumblebees
34. **And . . . thighs.** Make candles from the wax the bees produce
35. **I . . . mercy.** I beg your honor's pardon.
36. **I . . . acquaintance.** I hope to become better acquainted with you.
37. **If I cut . . . you.** Cobwebs were applied to wounds to stop the bleeding.

PEASEBLOSSOM. Peaseblossom.

BOTTOM. I pray you commend me to Mistress Squash, your mother, and to Master Peascod, your father. Good Master Peaseblossom, I shall desire you of more
180 acquaintance too. Your name, I beseech you, sir?

MUSTARDSEED. Mustardseed.

BOTTOM. Good Master Mustardseed, I know your patience well. That same cowardly, giant-like oxbeef hath devour'd many a gentleman of your house.[38] I
185 promise you your kindred hath made my eyes water ere now. I desire you of more acquaintance, good Master Mustardseed.

TITANIA. Come wait upon him; lead him to my <u>bower</u>. The moon methinks looks with a wat'ry eye;
190 And when she weeps, weeps every little flower, Lamenting some enforced[39] chastity. Tie up my lover's tongue, bring him silently.   *Exeunt.*

---

38. **That same . . . house.** Bottom is jesting about the way mustard is eaten with beef.
39. **enforced.** Violated

Words
For
Everyday
Use

bow • er (bou´ər) *n.*, place enclosed by overhanging boughs of trees

SCENE ii: The wood.

Enter King of Fairies (OBERON).

OBERON. I wonder if Titania be awak'd;
Then what it was that next came in her eye,
Which she must dote on in extremity.[1]

Enter PUCK.

Here comes my messenger. How now, mad spirit?
5   What night-rule[2] now about this haunted[3] grove?

PUCK. My mistress with a monster is in love.
Near to her close[4] and consecrated bower,
While she was in her dull and sleeping hour,
A crew of patches,[5] rude mechanicals,[6]
10   That work for bread upon Athenian stalls,
Were met together to rehearse a play
Intended for great Theseus' nuptial day.
The shallowest thick-skin of that barren sort,[7]
Who Pyramus presented, in their sport
15   Forsook his scene, and ent'red in a brake,
When I did him at this advantage take,
An ass's nole[8] I fixed on his head.
Anon his Thisby must be answered,
And forth my mimic[9] comes. When they him spy,
20   As wild geese that the creeping fowler[10] eye,
Or russet-pated choughs, many in sort[11]
(Rising and cawing at the gun's report),
Sever themselves and madly sweep the sky,
So, at his sight, away his fellows fly;
25   And at our stamp, here o'er and o'er one falls;
He murder cries, and help from Athens calls.

▶ *What does Puck think of the artisans he encountered?*

ACT III, SCENE ii
1. **in extremity.** To an extreme
2. **night-rule.** Happenings or events during the night
3. **haunted.** Often visited
4. **close.** Private
5. **crew of patches.** Groups of clowns or fools
6. **rude mechanicals.** Ignorant working-class people
7. **The shallowest . . . sort.** The stupidest member of the group of fools
8. **ass's nole.** Donkey's head
9. **mimic.** Actor
10. **fowler.** Person who hunts for birds
11. **Or . . . sort.** Or a flock of gray-headed jackdaws

Words
For
Everyday
Use

for • sake (fôr sāk´) *vt.,* leave; abandon

Their sense thus weak, lost with their fears thus strong,
Made senseless things begin to do them wrong,
For briers and thorns at their apparel snatch;
30 Some sleeves, some hats, from yielders all things catch.
I led them on in this distracted fear,
And left sweet Pyramus translated[12] there;
When in that moment (so it came to pass)
Titania wak'd, and straightway lov'd an ass.

35 OBERON. This falls out better than I could devise.[13]
But hast thou yet latch'd[14] the Athenian's eyes
With the love-juice, as I did bid thee do?

◄ *What is Oberon's opinion of the way Puck managed the situation with Titania?*

PUCK. I took him sleeping (that is finish'd too)
And the Athenian woman by his side
40 That when he wak'd, of force[15] she must be ey'd.

Enter DEMETRIUS *and* HERMIA.

OBERON. Stand close;[16] this is the same Athenian.

PUCK. This is the woman, but not this the man.

DEMETRIUS. O, why <u>rebuke</u> you him that loves you so?
Lay breath so bitter on your bitter foe.

45 HERMIA. Now I but <u>chide</u>; but I should use the worse
For thou (I fear) hast given me cause to curse.
If thou hast slain Lysander in his sleep,
Being o'er shoes in blood, plunge in the deep,
And kill me too.
50 The sun was not so true unto the day
As he to me. Would he have stolen away
From sleeping Hermia? I'll believe as soon
This whole earth may be bor'd,[17] and that the moon
May through the centre creep, and so displease
55 Her brother's[18] noontide with th' Antipodes.[19]
It cannot be but thou hast murd'red him;

◄ *What does Hermia believe that Demetrius has done? Why does she believe this?*

---

12. **translated.** Transformed
13. **devise.** Guess or imagine
14. **latch'd.** Moistened; dampened
15. **of force.** Necessarily
16. **close.** Concealed, hidden
17. **be bor'd.** Have a hole bored or drilled through it
18. **Her brother's.** The sun's
19. **Antipodes.** People who live on the opposite side of the earth

Words For Everyday Use

re • buke (ri byōōk´) *vt.*, blame or scold in a sharp way
chide (chīd) *vt.*, scold mildly

So should a murderer look—so dead,[20] so grim.

Demetrius. So should the murdered look, and so should I,
Pierc'd through the heart with your stern cruelty.
60 Yet you, the murderer, look as bright, as clear,
As yonder Venus in her glimmering sphere.

Hermia. What's this to my Lysander? Where is he?
Ah, good Demetrius, wilt thou give him me?

Demetrius. I had rather give his <u>carcass</u> to my hounds.

65 **Hermia.** Out, dog, out, cur! thou driv'st me past the bounds
Of maiden's patience. Hast thou slain him then?
Henceforth be never numb'red among men!
O, once tell true; tell true, even for my sake!
Durst thou have look'd upon him being awake?
70 And hast thou kill'd him sleeping? O brave touch![21]
Could not a worm, an adder,[22] do so much?
An adder did it! for with doubler tongue
Than thine, thou serpent, never adder stung.

▶ *Has Demetrius killed Lysander?*

Demetrius. You spend your passion on a mispris'd mood.[23]
75 I am not guilty of Lysander's blood;
Nor is he dead, for aught[24] that I can tell.

Hermia. I pray thee, tell me then that he is well.

Demetrius. And if I could, what should I get therefore?

Hermia. A privilege never to see me more.
80 And from thy hated presence part I so:
See me no more, whether he be dead or no.   *Exit.*

Demetrius. There is no following her in this fierce vein.[25]
Here therefore for a while I will remain.
So sorrow's heaviness doth heavier[26] grow

---

20. **dead.** Deathly pale
21. **brave touch.** Noble deed; Hermia is speaking ironically.
22. **adder.** Poisonous snake with a forked tongue
23. **You . . . a mispris'd mood.** Your anger is mistaken.
24. **aught.** All
25. **fierce vein.** Angry state of mind
26. **heavier.** Here means both "more serious in mood" and "sleepier"

Words
For
Everyday
Use

car • cass (kär′kəs) *n.,* human body, living or dead

85 For debt that bankrout sleep doth sorrow owe;[27]
   Which now in some slight measure it will pay,
   If for his tender[28] here I make some stay.

Lies down and sleeps.

◄ What does Oberon realize has occurred?

OBERON. What hast thou done? Thou hast mistaken quite
   And laid the love-juice on some true-love's sight.
90 Of thy misprision[29] must perforce[30] <u>ensue</u>
   Some true love turn'd, and not a false turn'd true.

PUCK. Then fate o'errules, that one man holding troth
   A million fail, confounding oath on oath.[31]

OBERON. About the wood go swifter than the wind,
95 And Helena of Athens look thou find.

◄ What does Oberon ask Puck to do to right the situation?

   All fancy-sick[32] she is and pale of cheer[33]
   With sighs of love, that costs the fresh blood dear.[34]
   By some illusion see thou bring her here.
   I'll charm his eyes against she do appear.[35]

100 PUCK. I go, I go, look how I go,
   Swifter than arrow from the Tartar's bow.   *Exit.*

OBERON. Flower of this purple dye,
      Hit with Cupid's archery,
      Sink in apple of his eye.[36]
105   When his love he doth espy,[37]
      Let her shine as gloriously
      As the Venus of the sky.
      When thou wak'st, if she[38] be by,
      Beg of her for remedy.

Enter PUCK.

110 PUCK.   Captain of our fairy band,
         Helena is here at hand

---

27. **For . . . owe.** Because sorrow has made me bankrupt of sleep
28. **If . . . tender.** Until sleep comes to collect its due
29. **misprision.** Mistake
30. **perforce.** Necessarily
31. **confounding . . . oath.** Breaking oath after oath
32. **fancy-sick.** Love-sick
33. **cheer.** Complexion
34. **sighs . . . dear.** Refers to the belief that each sigh costs the heart a drop of blood
35. **against . . . appear.** In preparation for her appearance
36. **apple of his eye.** Pupil; also any person or thing that one cherishes
37. **espy.** See
38. **she.** Venus, goddess of love

Words
For
Everyday
Use

en • sue (en sōō´) *vi.,* come afterward; follow immediately

▶ What amuses
Puck?

And the youth, mistook by me,
Pleading for a lover's fee.[39]
Shall we their fond pageant[40] see?
115 Lord, what fools these mortals be!

OBERON. Stand aside. The noise they make
Will cause Demetrius to awake.

PUCK. Then will two at once <u>woo</u> one;
That must needs be sport alone.[41]
120 And those things do best please me
That befall <u>prepost'rously</u>.

Enter LYSANDER *and* HELENA.

LYSANDER. Why should you think that I should woo in
scorn?
Scorn and <u>derision</u> never come in tears.
Look when I vow, I weep; and vows so born,
125 In their nativity all truth appears.[42]
How can these things in me seem scorn to you,
Bearing the badge of faith[43] to prove them true?

HELENA. You do advance your cunning more and more;
When truth kills truth, O devilish-holy <u>fray</u>!
130 These vows are Hermia's. Will you give her o'er?
Weigh oath with oath, and you will nothing weigh.
Your vows to her and me, put in two scales,
Will even weigh; and both as light as tales.

LYSANDER. I had no judgment when to her I swore.

135 **HELENA.** Nor none, in my mind, now you give her o'er.

LYSANDER. Demetrius loves her; and he loves not you.

DEMETRIUS. [*Awaking.*] O Helen, goddess, nymph,
perfect, divine!
To what, my love, shall I compare thine eyne?
Crystal is muddy. O, how ripe in show
140 Thy lips, those kissing cherries, tempting grow!

▶ What argument
does Lysander make
to plead his case
with Helena? What
does Demetrius
immediately do that
contradicts Lysander's
argument?

---

39. **fee.** Rights
40. **fond pageant.** Foolish exhibition or display
41. **sport alone.** Entertainment without equal; unique diversion
42. **vows . . . appears.** Vows that are made (or born) through tears reveal their sincerity in the nature of their birth
43. **badge of faith.** Tears

Words For Everyday Use

woo (wo͞o) *vt.*, try to get the love of; seek as a spouse
pre • pos • ter • ous • ly (prē päs′ tər əs lē) *adv.*, absurdly; contrary to nature
de • ri • sion (di rizh′ən) *n.*, contempt or ridicule
fray (frā) *n.*, noisy quarrel or fight

That pure congealed white, high Taurus'[44] snow,
Fann'd with the eastern wind, turns to a crow[45]
When thou hold'st up thy hand. O, let me kiss
This princess of pure white, this seal of bliss!

145 HELENA. O spite! O hell! I see you all are bent
To set against me for your merriment.
If you were civil and knew courtesy,
You would not do me thus much injury.
Can you not hate me, as I know you do,
150 But you must join in souls to mock me too?
If you were men, as men you are in show,[46]
You would not use a gentle[47] lady so;
To vow, and swear, and superpraise[48] my parts
When I am sure you hate me with your hearts.
155 You both are rivals, and love Hermia;
And now both rivals, to mock Helena.
A trim[49] exploit, a manly enterprise,
To conjure tears up in a poor maid's eyes
With your derision! None of noble sort
160 Would so offend a virgin, and extort[50]
A poor soul's patience, all to make you sport.

LYSANDER. You are unkind, Demetrius; be not so;
For you love Hermia; this you know I know.
And here, with all good will, with all my heart,
165 In Hermia's love I yield you up my part;
And yours of Helena to me <u>bequeath</u>,
Whom I do love, and will do till my death.

HELENA. Never did mockers waste more idle breath.

DEMETRIUS. Lysander, keep thy Hermia; I will none.
170 If e'er I lov'd her, all that love is gone.
My heart to her but as guest-wise sojourn'd,[51]
And now to Helen is it home return'd,
There to remain.

◄ What does
Helena believe
motivates both men's
praise of her?

◄ How does
Demetrius now feel
about Hermia?

---

44. **Taurus'.** Refers to a Turkish mountain range
45. **turns to a crow.** Seems as black as a crow's feathers
46. **in show.** In appearance; outwardly
47. **gentle.** Of noble birth
48. **superpraise.** Praise excessively
49. **trim.** Grand
50. **extort.** Wring out
51. **My heart . . . sojourn'd.** My heart visited with Hermia briefly, like a guest.

Words
For
Everyday
Use

be • queath (bē kwēth´) *vt.*, leave; pass on

LYSANDER.　　　　　　　　Helen, it is not so.

DEMETRIUS. <u>Disparage</u> not the faith thou dost not know,
175　Lest, to thy peril, thou aby it dear.[52]
Look where thy love comes; yonder is thy dear.

Enter HERMIA.

HERMIA. Dark night, that from the eye his[53] function takes,
The ear more quick of <u>apprehension</u> makes;
Wherein it doth <u>impair</u> the seeing sense,
180　It pays the hearing double <u>recompense</u>.
Thou art not by mine eye, Lysander, found;
Mine ear, I thank it, brought me to thy sound.
But why unkindly didst thou leave me so?

LYSANDER. Why should he stay, whom love doth press
　　to go?

185　**HERMIA.** What love could press Lysander from my side?

LYSANDER. Lysander's love, that would not let him <u>bide</u>—
Fair Helena! who more engilds[54] the night
Than all yon fiery oes[55] and eyes of light.
Why seek'st thou me? Could not this make thee know,
190　The hate I bare thee made me leave thee so?

HERMIA. You speak not as you think. It cannot be.

HELENA. Lo! she is one of this confederacy.
Now I perceive, they have conjoin'd all three
To fashion this false sport, in spite of me.
195　Injurious[56] Hermia, most ungrateful maid!
Have you conspir'd, have you with these contriv'd
To bait[57] me with this foul derision?
Is all the counsel that we two have shar'd,
The sisters' vows, the hours that we have spent,
200　When we have chid the hasty-footed time
For parting us—O, is all forgot?
All school-days friendship, childhood innocence?

▶ *What excuse does Lysander offer Hermia for leaving her? How do you think she feels about his response?*

▶ *In what way does Helena interpret this confusing situation?*

▶ *What time does Helena ask Hermia to recall? Why does Helena ask Hermia to remember this time?*

---

52. **aby it dear.** Pay dearly for it
53. **his.** Its
54. **engilds.** Makes bright, like gold
55. **oes.** Orbs; stars
56. **Injurious.** Insulting
57. **contriv'd . . . bait.** Planned or schemed to torment

We, Hermia, like two artificial[58] gods,
Have with our needles created both one flower,
205 Both on one sampler,[59] sitting on one cushion,
Both warbling of one song, both in one key,
As if our hands, our sides, voices, and minds
Had been incorporate.[60] So we grew together,
Like to a double cherry, seeming parted,
210 But yet an union in partition,
Two lovely berries molded on one stem;
So with two seeming bodies, but one heart,
Two of the first,[61] like coats in heraldry,[62]
Due but to one, and crowned with one crest.
215 And will you rent[63] our ancient love asunder,
To join with men in scorning your poor friend?
It is not friendly, 'tis not maidenly.
Our sex, as well as I, may chide you for it,
Though I alone do feel the injury.

220 HERMIA. I am amazed at your passionate words.
I scorn you not; it seems that you scorn me.

HELENA. Have you not set Lysander, as in scorn,
To follow me and praise my eyes and face?
And made your other love, Demetrius
225 (Who even but now did spurn me with his foot),
To call me goddess, nymph, divine and rare,
Precious, celestial? Wherefore[64] speaks he this
To her he hates? And wherefore doth Lysander
Deny your love[65] (so rich within his soul)
230 And tender[66] me (forsooth) affection,
But by your setting on, by your consent?
What though I be not so in grace[67] as you,
So hung upon with love, so fortunate

◄ Of what does
Helena accuse
Hermia?

---

58. **artificial.** Skilled in arts and crafts
59. **sampler.** Cloth embroidered with designs to show a beginner's skill
60. **incorporate.** United, as in one body
61. **first.** Refers to the bodies mentioned in the previous line
62. **coats in heraldry.** Emblems and figures usually arranged on and around a shield and serving as a special symbol of a person, family, or institution
63. **rent.** Tear
64. **Wherefore.** Why
65. **your love.** His love for you
66. **tender.** Offer
67. **grace.** Favor

Words
For
Everyday
Use

war • ble (wôr'bəl) vt., sing melodiously
a • sun • der (ə sun'dər) adv., into parts or pieces

(But miserable most, to love unlov'd)?
235 This you should pity rather than despise.

HERMIA. I understand not what you mean by this.

HELENA. Ay, do! persever,[68] <u>counterfeit</u> sad looks,
Make mouths[69] upon me when I turn my back,
Wink each at other, hold the sweet jest up;
240 This sport, well carried,[70] shall be <u>chronicled</u>.
If you have any pity, grace, or manners,
You would not make me such an argument.[71]
But fare ye well; 'tis partly my own fault,
Which death, or absence, soon shall remedy.

245 **LYSANDER.** Stay, gentle Helena; hear my excuse,
My love, my life, my soul, fair Helena!

HELENA. O excellent!

HERMIA.   Sweet, do not scorn her so.

DEMETRIUS. If she cannot entreat, I can compel.[72]

LYSANDER. Thou canst compel no more than she entreat.
250 Thy threats have no more strength than her weak prays.[73]
Helen, I love thee, by my life I do!
I swear by that[74] which I will lose for thee,
To prove him false that says I love thee not.

DEMETRIUS. I say I love thee more than he can do.

255 **LYSANDER.** If thou say so, withdraw, and prove it too.

DEMETRIUS. Quick, come!

HERMIA.   Lysander, whereto tends all this?

LYSANDER. Away, you Ethiop![75]

DEMETRIUS.   No, no; he'll
Seem to break loose—take on as you would follow,
But yet come not. You are a tame man, go!

---

68. **persever.** Persevere
69. **Make mouths.** Make faces
70. **carried.** Directed
71. **argument.** Topic or subject (of a cruel joke)
72. **If . . . compel.** If Hermia's words cannot move you to stop mocking Helena, I will force you to do so.
73. **prays.** Prayers, entreaties
74. **that.** My life
75. **Ethiop.** Moor, or person of North African and Arabic heritage; Lysander is referring scornfully to Hermia's dark hair.

| Words For Everyday Use | coun • ter • feit (kount´ər fit´) vt., make an imitation of to deceive |
| | chron • i • cle (krän´ i kəl) vt., tell or write the history of |

260 LYSANDER. Hang off,[76] thou cat, thou bur! Vile thing, let loose,
Or I will shake thee from me like a serpent!

HERMIA.   Why are you grown so rude? What change is this,
Sweet love?

LYSANDER.   Thy love? Out, tawny Tartar,[77] out!
Out, loathed med'cine! O hated potion, hence!

265 HERMIA.   Do you not jest?

HELENA.   Yes, sooth;[78] and so do you.

LYSANDER. Demetrius, I will keep my word[79] with thee.

DEMETRIUS.   I would I had your bond, for I perceive
A weak bond[80] holds you. I'll not trust your word.

LYSANDER. What? should I hurt her, strike her, kill her dead?
270 Although I hate her, I'll not harm her so.

HERMIA.   What? can you do me greater harm than hate?
Hate me, wherefore? O me, what news, my love!
Am not I Hermia? Are not you Lysander?
I am as fair now as I was erewhile.[81]

275 Since night you lov'd me; yet since night you left me:
Why then, you left me (O, the gods forbid!)
In earnest, shall I say?

LYSANDER.   Ay, by my life;
And never did desire to see thee more.
Therefore be out of hope, of question, of doubt;
280 Be certain! nothing truer; 'tis no jest
That I do hate thee, and love Helena.

HERMIA.   O me, you juggler, you canker-blossom,[82]
You thief of love! What, have you come by night
And stol'n my love's heart from him?

HELENA.   Fine, i' faith!
285 Have you no modesty, no maiden shame,
No touch of bashfulness? What, will you tear
Impatient answers from my gentle tongue?
Fie, fie, you counterfeit, you puppet,[83] you!

◄ In what way does Lysander behave toward Hermia?

◄ How does Hermia feel about the news that Lysander hates her?

◄ Of what does Hermia accuse Helena?

◄ In what way does Hermia believe Helena is insulting her? What does Hermia threaten to do to Helena?

---

76. **Hang off.** Let go (addressed to Hermia)
77. **tawny Tartar.** Brown barbarian (once again, Lysander is insulting Hermia's dark coloring, and alludes to her violent behavior)
78. **sooth.** In truth
79. **word.** Promise that I will fight you
80. **weak bond.** Hermia's arms. Demetrius implies Lysander is not trying very hard to escape.
81. **erewhile.** A short while before
82. **canker-blossom.** Worm that feeds on blossoms
83. **puppet.** Doll (contemptuous); Hermia takes this to be an insult about her height as she is short.

HERMIA. "Puppet"? Why so? Ay, that way goes the
    game.
290 Now I perceive that she hath made compare
    Between our <u>statures</u>: she hath urg'd her height,
    And with her personage, her tall personage,
    Her height, forsooth, she hath prevail'd with him.
    And are you grown so high in his esteem,
295 Because I am so dwarfish and so low?[84]
    How low am I, thou painted maypole?[85] Speak!
    How low am I? I am not yet so low
    But that my nails can reach unto thine eyes.

HELENA. I pray you, though you mock me, gentlemen,
300 Let her not hurt me. I was never curst;[86]
    I have no gift at all in shrewishness;
    I am a right[87] maid for my cowardice.
    Let her not strike me. You perhaps may think,
    Because she is something lower than myself,
305 That I can match her.

HERMIA.   "Lower"? hark[88] again.

HELENA. Good Hermia, do not be so bitter with me.
    I evermore did love you, Hermia,
    Did ever keep your counsels, never wrong'd you;
    Save that, in love unto Demetrius
310 I told him of your stealth[89] unto this wood.
    He followed you; for love I followed him.
    But he hath chid me hence, and threat'ned me
    To strike me, spurn me, nay, to kill me too.
    And now, so you will let me quiet go,
315 To Athens will I bear my folly back,
    And follow you no further. Let me go.
    You see how simple and how fond[90] I am.

HERMIA. Why, get you gone. Who is't that hinders you?

---

84. **low.** Short
85. **painted maypole.** Hermia is both insulting Helena's height and accusing
her of relying on makeup, then considered to be in poor taste.
86. **curst.** Cursed with a sharp tongue
87. **right.** True
88. **hark.** Listen (an exclamation)
89. **stealth.** Secret journey
90. **fond.** Foolish

Words
For
Everyday
Use

stat • ure (stach´ər) *n.,* height of a person

HELENA. A foolish heart, that I leave here behind.

320 HERMIA. What, with Lysander?

HELENA. With Demetrius.

LYSANDER. Be not afraid; she shall not harm thee, Helena.

DEMETRIUS. No, sir; she shall not, though you take her part.

HELENA. O, when she is angry, she is <u>keen</u> and shrewd![91]
She was a vixen[92] when she went to school;
325 And though she be but little, she is fierce.

HERMIA. "Little" again? Nothing but "low" and "little"?
Why will you suffer her to <u>flout</u> me thus?
Let me come to her.

LYSANDER. Get you gone, you dwarf;
You minimus,[93] of hind'ring knot-grass[94] made;
330 You bead, you acorn.

DEMETRIUS. You are too <u>officious</u>
In her behalf that scorns your services.
Let her alone; speak not of Helena,
Take not her part. For if thou dost intend
Never so little show of love to her,
335 Thou shalt aby it.[95]

LYSANDER. Now she holds me not;
Now follow, if thou dar'st, to try whose right,
Of thine or mine, is most in Helena.

DEMETRIUS. Follow? Nay; I'll go with thee, cheek by
jowl.[96]   *Exeunt* LYSANDER *and* DEMETRIUS.

HERMIA. You, mistress, all this coil is long of you.[97]
340 Nay, go not back.

◄ *What do Lysander and Demetrius plan to do?*

---

91. **shrewd.** Sharp-tongued; shrewish
92. **vixen.** Female fox; term used to describe an ill-tempered woman
93. **minimus.** TIny thing
94. **knot-grass.** Type of weed which was believed to hinder growth
95. **For . . . aby it.** If you offer Helena a pretense of love, you shall pay for it
96. **cheek by jowl.** At your side
97. **all . . . you.** All this commotion is because of you

Words For Everyday Use

keen (kēn) *adj.*, sharp or cutting
flout (flout) *vt.*, mock; show scorn or contempt for
of • fi • cious (ə fish´əs) *adj.*, offering unnecessary and unwanted advice; meddlesome

HELENA.   I will not trust you,
Nor longer stay in your curst company.
Your hands than mine are quicker for a fray;
My legs are longer though, to run away.   *Exit.*

HERMIA. I am amaz'd, and know not what to say.   *Exit.*

345 **OBERON.** This is thy negligence. Still[98] thou mistak'st,
Or else commit'st thy knaveries willfully.

PUCK. Believe me, king of shadows, I mistook.
Did not you tell me I should know the man
By the Athenian garments he had on?
350 And so far blameless proves my enterprise,
That I have 'nointed an Athenian's eyes;
And so far am I glad it so did sort,[99]
As this their jangling[100] I <u>esteem</u> a sport.

OBERON. Thou seest these lovers seek a place to fight;
355 Hie[101] therefore, Robin, overcast the night;
The starry welkin[102] cover thou anon
With drooping fog as black as Acheron,[103]
And lead these <u>testy</u> rivals so astray
As one come not within another's way.
360 Like to Lysander sometime frame thy tongue;[104]
Then stir Demetrius up with bitter wrong;[105]
And sometime <u>rail</u> thou like Demetrius;
And from each other look thou lead them thus,
Till o'er their brows death-counterfeiting sleep
365 With leaden legs and batty[106] wings doth creep.
Then crush this herb into Lysander's eye;
Whose liquor hath this virtuous[107] property,
To take from thence all error with his might,[108]
And make his eyeballs roll with <u>wonted</u> sight.

---

98. **Still.** Always, constantly
99. **sort.** Turn out
100. **jangling.** Arguing
101. **Hie.** Hurry
102. **welkin.** Vault of heaven; sky
103. **Acheron.** In Greek and Roman mythology, a river in Hades, the underworld
104. **Like . . . tongue.** Make your voice like Lysander's
105. **wrong.** Insult
106. **batty.** Batlike
107. **virtuous.** Potent
108. **with his might.** With it (the herb's) power

> ► What is Puck's attitude toward his mistake?

> ► What does Oberon ask Puck to do to prevent Lysander and Demetrius from fighting?

> ► What does Oberon ask Puck to do to right the situation among the four young Athenians?

| Words For Everyday Use | **es • teem** (e stēm) *vt.,* hold to be; consider; regard
tes • ty (tes′ tē) *adj.,* irritable; touchy
rail (rāl) *vi.,* speak bitterly or reproachfully
wont • ed (wänt′ id) *adj.,* customary; usual |

370 When they next wake, all this derision[109]
    Shall seem a dream and fruitless[110] vision,
    And back to Athens shall the lovers wend[111]
    With league whose date till death shall never end.[112]
    Whiles I in this affair do thee employ,
375 I'll to my queen and beg her Indian boy;
    And then I will her charmed eye release
    From monster's view, and all things shall be peace.

◄ How does Oberon plan to resolve his problems with his wife, Titania?

PUCK. My fairy lord, this must be done with haste,
    For Night's swift dragons cut the clouds full fast,
380 And yonder shines Aurora's harbinger,[113]
    At whose approach, ghosts, wand'ring here and there,
    Troop home to churchyards. Damned spirits all,
    That in crossways and floods have burial,
    Already to their wormy beds are gone.
385 For fear lest[114] day should look their shames upon,
    They willfully themselves exile from light,
    And must for aye consort with black-brow'd Night.

OBERON. But we are spirits of another sort.
    I with the Morning's love[115] have oft made sport,
390 And like a forester, the groves may tread
    Even till the eastern gate, all fiery red,
    Opening on Neptune[116] with fair blessed beams,
    Turns into yellow gold his salt green streams.
    But notwithstanding, haste, make no delay;
395 We may effect this business yet ere day.

PUCK. Up and down, up and down,
    I will lead them up and down;
    I am fear'd in field and town.
    Goblin, lead them up and down.
400 Here comes one.   *Exit.*

Enter LYSANDER.

LYSANDER. Where art thou, proud Demetrius? Speak
    thou now.

PUCK. Here, villain, drawn[117] and ready. Where art
    thou?

---

109. **derision.** Delusion
110. **fruitless.** Meaningless; insignificant
111. **wend.** Make their way
112. **With league . . . end.** Each couple joined together until death
113. **Aurora's harbinger.** The first sign of dawn; the morning star
114. **lest.** That
115. **Morning's love.** Refers to the goddess of dawn, Aurora, or to Aurora's beloved hunter, Cephalus
116. **Neptune.** God of the sea
117. **drawn.** With drawn sword

LYSANDER.   I will be with thee straight.[118]

PUCK.   Follow me then
To plainer[119] ground.

Exit LYSANDER, *as following the voice.*
Enter DEMETRIUS.

DEMETRIUS.   Lysander, speak again!
405 Thou runaway, thou coward, art thou fled?
Speak! In some bush? Where dost thou hide thy head?

PUCK.   Thou coward, art thou bragging to the stars,
Telling the bushes that thou look'st for wars,
And wilt not come? Come, <u>recreant</u>, come, thou child,
410 I'll whip thee with a rod. He is defil'd
That draws a sword on thee.

DEMETRIUS.   Yea, art thou there?

PUCK.   Follow my voice; we'll try no manhood[120] here.

                                    Exeunt.

Enter LYSANDER.

LYSANDER.   He goes before me, and still dares me on.
When I come where he calls, then he is gone.
415 The villain is much lighter-heel'd[121] than I;
I followed fast, but faster he did fly,
That fallen am I in dark uneven way,[122]
And here will rest me. [*Lies down.*] Come, thou gentle
     day!
For if but once thou show me thy gray light,
420 I'll find Demetrius and revenge this spite.   *Sleeps.*

Enter ROBIN (PUCK) *and* DEMETRIUS.

PUCK.   Ho, ho, ho! Coward, why com'st thou not?

DEMETRIUS.   Abide[123] me, if thou dar'st; for well I wot[124]
Thou run'st before me, shifting every place,
And dar'st not stand, nor look me in the face.
425 Where art thou now?

▶ *What does Lysander find frustrating about the chase on which Puck leads him?*

---

118. **straight.** Immediately
119. **plainer.** More open and clear
120. **we'll . . . manhood.** We will not test our bravery
121. **lighter-heel'd.** Swifter
122. **way.** Path
123. **Abide.** Await
124. **wot.** Know

Words
For
Everyday
Use

rec • re • ant (rek´rē ənt) *n*, coward; traitor

PUCK.   Come hither; I am here.

DEMETRIUS.   Nay then thou mock'st me. Thou shalt buy
     this dear,[125]
If ever I thy face by daylight see.
Now, go thy way. Faintness constraineth me
To measure out my length[126] on this cold bed.
430 By day's approach look to be visited.

                                        Lies down and sleeps.
Enter HELENA.

HELENA.   O weary night, O long and tedious night,
<u>Abate</u> thy hours! Shine, comforts, from the east,
That I may back to Athens by daylight,
From these that my poor company detest.
435 And sleep, that sometimes shuts up sorrow's eye,
Steal me a while from mine own company.   *Sleeps.*

PUCK.   Yet but three? Come one more;
          Two of both kinds makes up four.

Enter HERMIA.

          Here she comes, curst and sad.
440   Cupid is a knavish lad,
          Thus to make poor females mad.

HERMIA.   Never so weary, never so in woe,
Bedabbled[127] with the dew and torn with briers,
I can no further crawl, no further go;
445 My legs can keep no pace with my desires.
Here will I rest me till the break of day.
Heavens shield Lysander, if they mean a fray!

                                        Lies down and sleeps.

PUCK.   On the ground,
          Sleep sound;
450   I'll apply,
          To your eye,
Gentle lover, remedy.

                    Squeezing the juice on Lysander's eyes.
          When thou wak'st,

◄ *What does Puck do to Lysander? What effect will this have on him?*

---

125. **Thou . . . dear.** Pay dearly for this action
126. **measure . . . length.** Lie outstretched
127. **Bedabbled.** Smudged or smeared

Words For Everyday Use

a • bate (ə bāt´) *vt.*, make less in amount, degree, or force

              Thou tak'st
445   True delight
           In the sight
       Of thy former lady's eye;
       And the country <u>proverb</u> known,
       That every man should take his own,
460   In your waking shall be shown.
              Jack shall have Jill;
              Nought shall go ill:
       The man shall have his mare again, and all shall be well.

                                                        Exit.

Words
For
Everyday
Use

pro • verb (präv´ɚrb´) *n.,* short, traditional saying

56   *A MIDSUMMER NIGHT'S DREAM*

Responding to the Selection

In act III, scene ii, Puck exclaims, "Lord, what fools these mortals be!" Explain how the actions of the mortal characters in act III prove or disprove Puck's opinion.

Reviewing the Selection
Recalling and Interpreting

1. **R:** What problems do Bottom and the other artisans fear will arise from their intended performance? What solutions does Bottom devise? What does Puck do to interrupt this rehearsal? What happens when Bottom's singing awakens Titania? What does Bottom say in response to Titania's declaration of love and her praise of his wisdom and beauty?

2. **I:** Based on what you have seen of the noblewomen of Athens, explain whether the fears of Bottom and the other artisans about the play are justified. What do these fears reveal about the artisans as characters? about the artisans' perceptions about the theater? What do Bottom's solutions reveal about him? What do Bottom's responses to Titania reveal?

3. **R:** What does Oberon discover when he and Puck observe Lysander and Helena? What does Oberon order Puck to do to make amends for his mistake? What does Oberon do to Demetrius? What is the result of their actions?

4. **I:** How does Puck feel about his mistake and its results? How do Lysander, Demetrius, and Helena behave before Hermia enters? Why does Puck find mortal behavior so amusing?

5. **R:** When Hermia arrives, what does she ask Lysander? How does he respond? Why do Hermia and Helena fight? Why do Lysander and Demetrius fight?

6. **I:** How would you characterize the behavior of these four characters? Hermia asks Lysander, "Am not I Hermia? Are not you Lysander?" Why might she ask these questions? Explain whether the characters seem to have a "midsummer madness."

7. **R:** What does Oberon order Puck to do to end the strife among the four young Athenians? From whom does Puck lift the enchantment? On whom does the enchantment remain? What does Puck promise at the very end of act III?

8. **I:** Why does Oberon leave this character enchanted? Explain whether harmony among the four young Athenians would be possible without the aid of Oberon's magic. What does this reveal about the fairies' role in the natural world? Explain whether you think it is fair for Oberon to leave one of the characters enchanted. Do you think that the situation will be resolved as Puck promises? Why, or why not?

Synthesizing

9. Many characters in act III experience transformations. Which characters have experienced physical transformations and which have experienced inner, or emotional, changes? Compare and contrast the characters who undergo these two different types of transformation. What change seems to create more difficulty for a person?

10. Dreams and the theater are two important themes in this play. What events in act III seem particularly dreamlike? What view of the theater is presented in act III? What is Bottom trying to do to the illusions in the play he is to perform? How might stripping a play of its illusions affect the play as a whole? In what way might dreams and the theater be related or interdependent?

Understanding Literature (QUESTIONS FOR DISCUSSION)

1. **Character.** A **character** is a person (or sometimes an animal) who figures in the action of a literary work. Many writers have used the device of the **doppelgänger**, or a character's double, to point out similarities between the two. When you were reading act III, were you ever confused about which character was which? Find examples of passages in acts I, II, and III in which Lysander and Demetrius are portrayed as doubles or doppelgängers or in which Hermia and Helena are portrayed in this way. Why might Shakespeare have made these characters so similar? Explain whether the four young Athenians are fully developed as characters. In what way does the use of doppelgängers affect the confusion of identity that takes place in act III?

2. **Dramatic Irony and Pun.** In **dramatic irony** something is known by the reader or audience but unknown to the characters. A **pun** is a play on words, one that wittily exploits a double meaning. Many of the puns that would have been readily understood by Shakespeare's audience have become more obscure to a modern audience. When Snout comments on Bottom's transformation, Bottom responds, "What do you see? You see an ass-head of your own, do you?" Look at the footnote for this line. Then explain how Bottom's response is a pun. What dramatic irony is involved in his response? In other words, of what is Bottom unaware?

3. **Climax and Crisis.** The **climax** is the point of highest interest and suspense in a literary work. The **crisis**, or **turning point**, often the same event as the climax, is the point in the plot where something decisive happens to determine the future course of events. What is the crisis that occurs in act III? In what way does the action build to a climax during this act? In what way do things become worse before they become better?

Act IV

SCENE i: Scene continues.

Enter Queen of Fairies (TITANIA) *and Clown* (BOTTOM), *and Fairies* (PEASEBLOSSOM, COBWEB, MOTH, MUSTARDSEED, *and others, attending); and the King* (OBERON) *behind them unseen.*

TITANIA.   Come sit thee down upon this flow'ry bed,
While I thy amiable cheeks do coy,[1]
And stick musk-roses in thy sleek smooth head,
And kiss thy fair large ears, my gentle joy.

5   BOTTOM.   Where's Peaseblossom?

PEASEBLOSSOM.   Ready.

BOTTOM.   Scratch my head, Peaseblossom. Where's Mounsieur Cobweb?

COBWEB.   Ready.

10   BOTTOM.   Mounsieur Cobweb, good mounsieur, get you your weapons in your hand, and kill me a red-hipp'd humble-bee on the top of a thistle; and, good mounsieur, bring me the honey-bag. Do not fret yourself too much in the action, mounsieur; and, good mounsieur, have a
15   care the honey-bag break not, I would be <u>loath</u> to have you overflowen with a honey-bag, signior.[2] Where's Mounsieur Mustardseed?

MUSTARDSEED.   Ready.

BOTTOM.   Give me your neaf,[3] Mounsieur Mustardseed.
20   Pray you, leave your curtsy, good mounsieur.

MUSTARDSEED.   What's your will?

BOTTOM.   Nothing, good mounsieur, but to help Cavalery[4] Cobweb to scratch. I must to the barber's, mounsieur; for methinks I am marvail's[5] hairy about the
25   face; and I am such a tender ass, if my hair do but tickle me, I must scratch.

◄ *What one sign of his transformation has Bottom noticed?*

ACT IV, SCENE i
1. **coy.** Caress
2. **signior.** Mr., an Italian title of respect
3. **neaf.** Hand
4. **Cavalery.** Cavalier
5. **marvail's.** Marvelous

Words For Everyday Use   **loath** (lōth) *adj.,* unwilling; reluctant

TITANIA. What, wilt thou hear some music, my sweet love?

BOTTOM. I have a reasonable good ear in music. Let's have the tongs and the bones.[6]

Music. Tongs. Rural music.

30 TITANIA. Or say, sweet love, what thou desirest to eat.

► What does Bottom wish to eat?

BOTTOM. Truly, a peck of provender;[7] I could munch your good dry oats. Methinks I have a great desire to a bottle[8] of hay. Good hay, sweet hay, hath no fellow.

TITANIA. I have a <u>venturous</u> fairy that shall seek
35 The squirrel's hoard, and fetch thee new nuts.

BOTTOM. I had rather have a handful or two of dried peas. But, I pray you, let none of your people stir me; I have an exposition[9] of sleep come upon me.

TITANIA. Sleep thou, and I will wind thee in my arms.
40 Fairies, be gone, and be all ways[10] away.

Exeunt FAIRIES.

So doth the woodbine the sweet honeysuckle
Gently entwist; the female ivy so
Enrings the barky[11] fingers of the elm.
O, how I love thee! how I dote on thee!   *They sleep.*

Enter ROBIN GOODFELLOW (PUCK).

► How is Oberon beginning to feel about Titania and her charmed love for Bottom?

45 OBERON. [*Advancing.*] Welcome, good Robin. Seest thou this sweet sight?
Her dotage now I do begin to pity.
For meeting her of late behind the wood
Seeking sweet favors[12] for this hateful fool,
I did <u>upbraid</u> her, and fall out[13] with her.
50 For she his hairy temples then had rounded
With coronet of fresh and fragrant flowers;

---

6. **the tongs and the bones.** Tongs and bones are musical instruments most often used in rustic areas.
7. **peck of provender.** One quarter-bushel of dry food for livestock
8. **bottle.** Bundle
9. **exposition.** Another verbal mistake; Bottom means "disposition," i.e. "desire."
10. **all ways.** In different directions
11. **barky.** Bark-covered
12. **favors.** Flowers as gifts
13. **fall out.** Had a disagreement

Words For Everyday Use	**ven • tur • ous** (ven´chər əs) *adj.,* daring; inclined to take chances **up • braid** (up brād´) *vt.,* rebuke severely or bitterly

And that same dew which sometime on the buds
Was wont[14] to swell like round and orient[15] pearls,
Stood now within the pretty flouriets'[16] eyes,
55   Like tears that did their own disgrace bewail.
When I had at my pleasure taunted her,
And she in mild terms begg'd my patience
I then did ask of her her changeling child;
Which straight she gave me, and her fairy sent
60   To bear him to my bower in fairy land.
And now I have the boy, I will undo
This hateful imperfection of her eyes.
And, gentle Puck, take this transformed scalp[17]
From off the head of this Athenian swain,[18]
65   That he, awaking when the other[19] do,
May all to Athens back again repair,
And think no more of this night's accidents[20]
But as the fierce vexation of a dream.
But first I will release the Fairy Queen.

Touching her eyes.

70   Be as thou wast wont to be;
        See as thou wast wont to see.
        Dian's bud o'er Cupid's flower
        Hath such force and blessed power.

Now, my Titania, wake you, my sweet queen.

75   TITANIA.   My Oberon, what visions have I seen!
Methought I was enamor'd of an ass.

OBERON.   There lies your love.

TITANIA.   How came these things to pass?
O, how mine eyes do loathe his visage now!

OBERON.   Silence a while. Robin, take off this head.
80   Titania, music call, and strike more dead
Than common sleep of all these five the sense.[21]

TITANIA.   Music, ho, music, such as charmeth sleep!

Music, still.[22]

◄ *What has Titania given Oberon? What is Oberon now willing to do?*

◄ *According to Oberon, in what way will the Athenians interpret their experiences when they awaken?*

---

14. **wont.** Accustomed
15. **orient.** Lustrous; quality that determines a pearl's value
16. **flouriets'.** Flowers'
17. **scalp.** Refers to the ass's head
18. **swain.** Country youth
19. **other.** Others
20. **accidents.** Happenings
21. **strike . . . sense.** Put Lysander, Hermia, Demetrius, Helena, and Bottom into a sleep that is much deeper than is usual.
22. *Music, still.* Quiet music

PUCK. Now, when thou wak'st, with thine own fool's
eyes peep.

► What condition
exists again between
Oberon and Titania?
What do they plan to
do the following
night? Who else will
be wedded the
following night?

OBERON. Sound, music! [*Louder music.*] Come, my
queen, take hands with me,
85 And rock the ground whereon these sleepers be.
Now thou and I are new in <u>amity</u>,
And will tomorrow midnight solemnly[23]
Dance in Duke Theseus' house triumphantly[24]
And bless it to all fair <u>prosperity</u>.
90 There shall the pairs of faithful lovers be
Wedded, with Theseus, all in <u>jollity</u>.

PUCK. Fairy King, attend and mark;
I do hear the morning lark.

OBERON. Then, my queen, in silence sad,[25]
95 Trip[26] we after night's shade.
We the globe can compass[27] soon,
Swifter than the wand'ring moon.

TITANIA. Come, my lord, and in our flight,
Tell me how it came this night
100 That I sleeping here was found,
With these mortals on the ground.

Exeunt. Wind[28] horn within.

Enter THESEUS, HIPPOLYTA, EGEUS, *and all his* TRAIN.

THESEUS. Go, one of you, find out the forester,
For now our observation is perform'd,
And since we have the vaward[29] of the day,

► How do Theseus
and Hippolyta plan to
pass their morning?

105 My love shall hear the music of my hounds.
Uncouple[30] in the western valley, let them go.
<u>Dispatch</u>, I say, and find the forester.

Exit an ATTENDANT.

---

23. **solemnly.** Formally
24. **triumphantly.** In part of a public celebration
25. **sad.** Solemn
26. **Trip.** Walk, run, or dance with light steps
27. **compass.** Go around
28. **Wind.** Blow
29. **vaward.** Early portion
30. **Uncouple.** Set them free; unleash them

| Words
For
Everyday
Use | am • i • ty (am´i tē) *n.*, friendship
pros • per • i • ty (prä sper´ə tē) *n.*,
good fortune, wealth, and success | jol • li • ty (jäl´ə tē) *n.*, state of high
spirits and good humor
dis • patch (di spach´) *vt.*, send off or
out promptly |

We will, fair queen, up to the mountain's top,
And mark the musical confusion
110 Of hounds and echo in <u>conjunction</u>.

HIPPOLYTA. I was with Hercules and Cadmus[31] once,
When in a wood of Crete they bay'd[32] the bear
With hounds of Sparta. Never did I hear
Such gallant chiding;[33] for besides the groves,
115 The skies, the fountains, every region near
Seem all one mutual cry. I never heard
So musical a <u>discord</u>, such sweet thunder.

THESEUS. My hounds are bred out of the Spartan kind;
So flew'd, so sanded;[34] and their heads are hung
120 With ears that sweep away the morning dew;
Crook-knee'd, and dewlapp'd[35] like Thessalian[36] bulls;
Slow in pursuit; but match'd in mouth like bells,
Each under each.[37] A cry more tuneable
Was never hollow'd to,[38] nor cheer'd with horn,
125 In Crete, in Sparta, nor in Thessaly.
Judge when you hear. But soft![39] What nymphs these?

EGEUS. My lord, this my daughter here asleep,
And this Lysander, this Demetrius is,
This Helena, old Nedar's Helena.
130 I wonder of their being here together.

THESEUS. No doubt they rose up early to observe
The rite of May; and hearing our intent,
Came here in grace of our solemnity.[40]
But speak, Egeus, is not this the day
135 That Hermia should give answer of her choice?

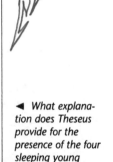

◄ *What explanation does Theseus provide for the presence of the four sleeping young people? Is he correct?*

---

31. **Hercules and Cadmus.** Hercules and Cadmus are both heroes of Greek legend; Hercules was renowned for his strength and Cadmus was the legendary founder of Thebes
32. **bay'd.** Cornered; forced into a situation that makes escape impossible
33. **chiding.** Baying; barking
34. **So . . . sanded.** With flaps of skin hanging from their lower cheeks and sandy in color
35. **dewlapp'd.** Having a flap of skin beneath the chin
36. **Thessalian.** From Thessaly, a region in eastern Greece
37. **match'd . . . each.** With voices like bells of different tones
38. **hollow'd to.** Urged on hounds by shouting out "hollo"
39. **soft.** Wait; stop
40. **in . . . solemnity.** In honor of our observation of the rites of May

Words
For
Everyday
Use

con • junc • tion (kən juŋk´shən) *n.*, a joining together; union

dis • cord (dis´kôrd) *n.*, inharmonious combination of tones sounded together

EGEUS. It is, my lord.

THESEUS. Go, bid the huntsmen wake them with their
    horns.
Exit an ATTENDANT. *Shout within. Wind horns. They all start
    up.*
Good morrow, friends. Saint Valentine is past;
Begin these wood-birds but to couple now?[41]

140 LYSANDER. Pardon, my lord.   *They kneel.*

THESEUS.   I pray you all, stand up.
I know you two are rival enemies.
How comes this gentle <u>concord</u> in the world,
That hatred is so far from jealousy[42]
To sleep by hate[43] and fear no <u>enmity</u>?

▶ Of what is
Lysander unsure?
What does he
remember?

145 LYSANDER. My lord, I shall reply amazedly,[44]
Half sleep, half waking; but, as yet, I swear,
I cannot truly say how I came here.
But, as I think—for truly would I speak,
And now I do bethink me, so it is—
150 I came with Hermia hither. Our intent
Was to be gone from Athens, where we might,
Without the peril of the Athenian law—

EGEUS. Enough, enough, my lord; you have enough.
I beg the law, the law, upon his head.
155 They would have stol'n away, they would, Demetrius
Thereby to have defeated you and me:
You of your wife, and me of my consent,
Of my consent that she should be your wife.

DEMETRIUS. My lord, fair Helen told me of their stealth,
160 Of this their purpose hither to this wood,
And I in fury hither followed them,
Fair Helena in fancy[45] following me.

▶ What does
Demetrius tell Egeus
about his feelings?

But, my good lord, I wot not by what power
(But by some power it is), my love to Hermia

---

41. **Saint . . . now.** Refers to a contemporary belief that birds chose their
partners on February 14, Saint Valentine's Day
42. **jealousy.** Resentful suspicion
43. **hate.** One whom you hate
44. **amazedly.** With confusion
45. **fancy.** Love

Words For Everyday Use	**con • cord** (kän´ kôrd) *n.,* agreement; harmony
	en • mi • ty (en´mə tē) *n.,* hostility

165 (Melted as the snow) seems to me now
As the remembrance of an idle gaud,[46]
Which in my childhood I did dote upon;
And all the faith, the virtue of my heart,
The object and the pleasure of mine eye,
170 Is only Helena. To her, my lord,
Was I betrothed[47] ere I saw Hermia;
But like a sickness did I loathe this food;
But, as in health, come to my natural taste,
Now I do wish it, love it, long for it,
175 And will for evermore be true to it.

THESEUS.   Fair lovers, you are fortunately met;
Of this discourse we more will hear anon.
Egeus, I will overbear[48] your will;
For in the temple, by and by, with us
180 These couples shall eternally be knit.
And, for the morning now is something worn,
Our purpos'd hunting shall be set aside.
Away with us to Athens. Three and three,
We'll hold a feast in great solemnity.
185 Come, Hippolyta.

                 Exeunt THESEUS, HIPPOLYTA, EGEUS, *and* TRAIN.

DEMETRIUS.   These things seem small and
      undistinguishable,
Like far-off mountains turned into clouds.

HERMIA.   Methinks I see these things with parted[49]
      eye,
When every thing seems double.

HELENA.   So methinks;
190 And I have found Demetrius like a jewel,
Mine own, and not mine own.

DEMETRIUS.   Are you sure
That we are awake? It seems to me
That yet we sleep, we dream. Do not you think
The Duke was here, and bid us follow him?

195 HERMIA.   Yea, and my father.

HELENA.   And Hippolyta.

LYSANDER.   And he did bid us follow to the temple.

◄ What is Theseus's final decision about the matter brought before him by Egeus?

◄ What are the young people having a hard time doing upon awakening?

◄ About what aren't the four young people sure? How does Demetrius describe their condition? What do they decide to do on their way to the temple?

---

46. **idle gaud.** Cheap, showy trinket
47. **betrothed.** Engaged to be wed
48. **overbear.** Overrule
49. **parted.** Unfocused

DEMETRIUS. Why then, we are awake. Let's follow him,
And by the way let's <u>recount</u> our dreams.

Exeunt LOVERS.

BOTTOM. [*Awaking.*] When my cue comes, call me, and
200 I will answer. My next is, "Most fair Pyramus."
Heighho! Peter Quince! Flute the bellows-mender!
Snout the tinker! Starveling! God's my life,[50] stol'n
hence, and left me asleep! I have had a most rare
vision. I have had a dream, past the wit of man to say
205 what dream it was. Man is but an ass, if he go about t'
<u>expound</u> this dream. Methought I was—there is no
man can tell what. Methought I was, and methought I
had—but man is but a patch'd[51] fool, if he will offer to
say what methought I had. The eye of man hath not
210 heard, the ear of man hath not seen, man's hand is not
able to taste, his tongue to conceive, nor his heart to
report, what my dream was. I will get Peter Quince to
write a ballet[52] of this dream. It shall be call'd
215 "Bottom's Dream," because it hath no bottom; and I
will sing it in the latter end of a play, before the Duke.
Peradventure,[53] to make it the more gracious, I shall
sing it at her[54] death.   *Exit.*

SCENE ii: Quince's house.

Enter QUINCE, *Thisby* (FLUTE), *and the rabble* (SNOUT,
STARVELING).

QUINCE. Have you sent to Bottom's house? Is he come
home yet?

STARVELING. He cannot be heard of. Out of doubt he is
transported.[1]

5 FLUTE. If he come not, then the play is marr'd. It
goes not forward, doth it?

---

50. **God's . . . life.** Oath
51. **patch'd.** Refers to the patchwork of traditional jester's or fool's clothing
52. **ballet.** Ballad
53. **Peradventure.** Perhaps
54. **her.** Thisbe's
ACT IV, SCENE ii
1. **transported.** Carried away by fairies

Words
For
Everyday
Use

re • **count** (ri kount´) *vt.,* tell in detail
ex • **pound** (eks pound´) *vt.,* explain or interpret

▶ In what way does
Bottom interpret his
experiences in the
wood?

▶ What does
Bottom plan to do
with all that he has
experienced?

▶ What opinion do
the other artisans
hold of Bottom?
What do they say
they cannot do
without him?

QUINCE. It is not possible. You have not a man in all Athens able to discharge[2] Pyramus but he.

FLUTE. No, he hath simply the best wit of an handicraft man in Athens.

QUINCE. Yea, and the best person too; and he is a very paramour[3] for a sweet voice.

FLUTE. You must say "paragon." A paramour is (God bless us!) a thing of naught.[4]

Enter SNUG the joiner.

SNUG. Masters, the Duke is coming from the temple, and there is two or three lords and ladies more married. If our sport had gone forward, we had all been made[5] men.

FLUTE. O sweet bully Bottom! Thus hath he lost sixpence a day during his life;[6] he could not have scap'd[7] sixpence a day. And the Duke had not given him sixpence a day for playing Pyramus, I'll be hang'd. He would have deserv'd it. Sixpence a day in Pyramus, or nothing.

Enter BOTTOM.

BOTTOM. Where are these lads? Where are these hearts?

QUINCE. Bottom! O most courageous day! O most happy hour!

BOTTOM. Masters, I am to discourse[8] wonders; but ask me not what; for if I tell you, I am no true Athenian. I will tell you every thing, right as it fell out.

◄ *What does Bottom say he will do? Does he do this?*

QUINCE. Let us hear, sweet Bottom.

BOTTOM. Not a word of me. All that I will tell you is, that the Duke hath din'd. Get your apparel together,

---

2. **discharge.** Play the role of
3. **paramour.** Lover; illicit romantic partner
4. **naught.** Wickedness
5. **made.** Successful; fortunate
6. **sixpence . . . life.** Flute is saying that he believes that Bottom would have been given a royal pension because of his dramatic ability.
7. **scap'd.** Been rewarded less than
8. **discourse.** Relate, reveal

Words
For
Everyday
Use

par • a • gon (par´ə gän´) *n.,* model or pattern of perfection or excellence

▶ *What news does Bottom bring?*

35 good strings to your beards, new ribands to your pumps;[9] meet presently at the palace; every man look o'er his part; for the short and the long is, our play is preferr'd.[10] In any case, let Thisby have clean linen; and let not him that plays the lion pare[11] his nails, for they shall hang
40 out for the lion's claws. And, most dear actors, eat no onions nor garlic, for we are to utter sweet breath; and I do not doubt but to hear them say, it is a sweet comedy. No more words. Away, go, away!   *Exeunt.*

---

9. **ribands . . . pumps.** Ribbons for your shoes
10. **preferr'd.** Given preference or priority
11. **pare.** Cut

Responding to the Selection

Think about a time when you had a dream that was so vivid it seemed real. About what did you dream? When you awoke, were you unable for a brief moment to tell the difference between reality and your dream? If so, describe how this experience felt. If not, describe another situation in which you had difficulty telling what was real and what was imagined.

Reviewing the Selection

Recalling and Interpreting

1. **R:** What sort of treatment is Bottom enjoying among the fairies? What does Bottom notice about his face? What type of food does he crave?

2. **I:** Explain whether you think Bottom is accustomed to such treatment. How does he respond to it? Explain whether Bottom is aware of his transformation. What does his knowledge or lack of knowledge indicate about him as a character? In what way does it contribute to the humor of the opening of act IV?

3. **R:** How does Oberon now feel about Titania's condition? From what does he release her? What does he order Puck to do for Bottom? What is the final thing the fairies do to the mortals?

4. **I:** Explain why Oberon's feelings have changed. Would you describe him as a gracious winner? Why, or why not? Why isn't Titiana angry with Oberon? What might her reaction indicate about the view of gender and authority presented? Why do the fairies do this final thing to the mortals? Why might it be important for the mortals to think of their experiences as dreams?

5. **R:** What are Theseus and Hippolyta planning to do when they encounter the sleeping Athenians? What is unusual about Theseus's hounds? What does Lysander say that angers Egeus? What does Demetrius tell Egeus? In what way does Theseus put an end to the conflict Egeus introduced at the play's beginning?

6. **I:** In what way does the unusual nature of these hounds reflect the harmony and reestablishment of order and authority that takes place in act IV? Why is Theseus now willing to tell Egeus, "I will overbear your will," when he was unwilling or unable to "extenuate" the law at the play's beginning?

7. **R:** What are the other artisans unable to do without Bottom? What is their opinion of him? What news does Bottom bring them?

8. **I:** Explain whether Bottom deserves the other artisans' high opinion of him. Does Bottom himself share in their opinion? Predict what you think the artisans' play will be like.

Synthesizing

9. In what way are the four young Athenians' perceptions altered when they awake? With what are they having difficulty? Explain what questions about dreams and reality their experiences raise. Compare and contrast these characters' reactions as they wake to Bottom's reaction. How does Bottom respond to his experiences?

10. Most comedies progress from order to disorder and back to order again. Explain whether this pattern is followed in each of the following elements of the play: in the natural world, in the fairies' world, in the romantic world of the four young Athenians, in the relationship between father (Egeus) and daughter (Hermia), and in the political world of Theseus's Athens.

Understanding Literature (QUESTIONS FOR DISCUSSION)

1. Synaesthesia and Pun. Synaesthesia is a figure of speech that combines in a single expression images related to two or more different senses. A **pun** is a play on words, one that wittily exploits a double meaning. Examine Bottom's speech when he awakens at the end of act IV, scene i. What examples of synaesthesia appear in this speech? Why do you think Shakespeare chose to use this technique in this particular speech? Bottom intends for Peter Quince to write a ballad about his dream and that "It shall be call'd 'Bottom's Dream,' because it hath no bottom." Explain the pun on the word *bottom*. What is Bottom indicating about his dream? In what way is Bottom's intent similar to Shakespeare's intent in writing *A Midsummer Night's Dream*? Explain whether "Bottom's Dream" could be an appropriate title for *A Midsummer Night's Dream*. When does Bottom wish to recite his dream? If he were to do so, what effect would this have on the play—not the artisans' intended performance but *A Midsummer Night's Dream* itself?

2. Simile. A **simile** is a comparison using *like* or *as*. A simile can be divided into two parts, the **tenor** (or subject being described), and the **vehicle** (or object being used in the description). Helena says, "I have found Demetrius like a jewel, / Mine own, and not mine own." In this simile, what is the tenor? What is the vehicle? What does Helena mean by "Mine own, and not mine own"? In what way are the jewel and the man alike? What simile does Demetrius use to describe how his feelings changed from love for Helena to loathing and back again?

Act V

SCENE i: Athens. The palace of Theseus.

Enter THESEUS, HIPPOLYTA, *and* PHILOSTRATE, LORDS, *and*
ATTENDANTS.

HIPPOLYTA. 'Tis strange, my Theseus, that these lovers
   speak of.

THESEUS.   More strange than true. I never may believe
These antic[1] fables, nor these fairy toys.[2]
Lovers and madmen have such <u>seething</u> brains,
5   Such shaping fantasies,[3] that apprehend
More than cool reason ever comprehends.
The lunatic, the lover, and the poet
Are of imagination all compact.[4]
One sees more devils than vast hell can hold;
10   That is the madman. The lover, all as frantic,
Sees Helen's beauty in a brow of Egypt.[5]
The poet's eye, in a fine <u>frenzy</u> rolling,
Doth glance from heaven to earth, from earth to heaven;
And as imagination bodies forth
15   The forms of things unknown, the poet's pen
Turns them to shapes, and gives to aery[6] nothing
A local <u>habitation</u> and a name.
Such tricks hath strong imagination,
That if it would but apprehend some joy,
20   It comprehends some bringer of that joy;[7]
Or in the night, imagining some fear,
How easy is a bush suppos'd a bear!

HIPPOLYTA.   But all the story of the night told over,
And all their minds <u>transfigur'd</u> so together,
25   More witnesseth than fancy's images,[8]

◄ *What is Theseus's
opinion of the young
lovers' strange tale?
Why does he feel this
way?*

◄ *According to
Theseus, in what
ways are lunatics,
lovers, and poets
alike?*

◄ *What is
Hippolyta's opinion
of the lovers' story?*

ACT V, SCENE i
  1. **antic.** Ludicrous; silly
  2. **fairy toys.** Frivolous stories about fairies
  3. **shaping fantasies.** Easily shaped or influenced imaginations
  4. **compact.** Composed
  5. **Sees . . . Egypt.** Sees the beauty of Helen of Troy, considered the most
beautiful woman in the world, in a gypsy's brow
  6. **aery.** Airy
  7. **That if . . . joy.** If the imagination perceives a joy, it also imagines someone
who brings this joy.
  8. **More . . . images.** Gives evidence of more than imaginary notions and ideas

| Words For Everyday Use | seeth • ing (sēth´iŋ) *adj.,* boiling; violently agitated | hab • i • ta • tion (hab´i tā´shən) *n.,* place in which to live |
| | fren • zy (fren´zē) *n.,* wild outburst of feeling or action | trans • fig • ure (trans fig´yər) *vt.,* transform |

And grows to something of great constancy;[9]
But howsoever, strange and admirable.[10]

Enter lovers, LYSANDER, DEMETRIUS, HERMIA, *and* HELENA.

THESEUS.   Here come the lovers, full of joy and <u>mirth</u>.
Joy, gentle friends, joy and fresh days of love
30   Accompany your hearts!

LYSANDER.   More[11] than to us
Wait in your royal walks, your board,[12] your bed!

THESEUS.   Come now; what <u>masques</u>, what dances shall
      we have,
To wear away this long age of three hours
Between our after-supper and bed-time?
35   Where is our usual manager of mirth?
What revels are in hand? Is there no play
To ease the anguish of a torturing hour?
Call Philostrate.

PHILOSTRATE.   Here, mighty Theseus.

<table><tr><td>► *What is Theseus going to choose?*</td><td>THESEUS.   Say, what abridgment[13] have you for this evening?</td></tr></table>

40   What masque? what music? How shall we beguile
The lazy time, if not with some delight?

PHILOSTRATE.   There is a brief how many sports are
      ripe.[14]
Make choice of which your Highness will see first.
                                        Giving a paper.

THESEUS.   [*Reads.*] "The battle with the Centaurs,[15] to be
      sung
45   By an Athenian eunuch[16] to the harp."
We'll none of that: that have I told my love,
In glory of my kinsman Hercules.
"The riot of the tipsy Bacchanals,

---

9. **constancy.** Certainty
10. **admirable.** Inspiring wonder
11. **More.** More joys
12. **board.** Table
13. **abridgment.** Amusement; diversion
14. **brief . . . ripe.** List of entertainments that are ready to be presented
15. **battle . . . Centaurs.** Story about a battle that takes place when centaurs, half human and half horse, try to kidnap the bride from a wedding
16. **eunuch.** Emasculated man

Words
For
Everyday
Use

mirth (mʉrth) *n.*, joyfulness and merriment characterized by laughter
masque (mask) *n.*, dramatic entertainment popular among the aristocracy of the sixteenth and seventeenth centuries, usually based on a mythical or allegorical theme and featuring lavish costumes, scenery, dancing, and music

Tearing the Thracian singer in their rage."[17]
50 That is an old device; and it was play'd
When I from Thebes came last a conqueror.
"The thrice three Muses mourning for the death
Of Learning, late deceas'd in beggary."
That is some satire, keen and critical,
55 Not sorting with[18] a nuptial ceremony.
"A <u>tedious</u> brief scene of young Pyramus
And his love Thisby; very tragical mirth."
Merry and tragical? Tedious and brief?
That is hot ice and wondrous strange snow.
60 How shall we find the concord of this discord?

PHILOSTRATE.   A play there is, my lord, some ten words
     long,
Which is as brief as I have known a play;
But by ten words, my lord, it is too long,
Which makes it tedious; for in all the play
65 There is not one word <u>apt</u>, one player fitted.[19]
And tragical, my noble lord, it is;
For Pyramus therein doth kill himself;
Which when I saw rehears'd, I must confess,
Made mine eyes water; but more merry tears
70 The passion of loud laughter never shed.

THESEUS.   What are they that do play it?

PHILOSTRATE.   Hard-handed men that work in Athens
     here,
Which never labor'd in their minds till now;
And now have toiled their unbreathed[20] memories
75 With this same play, against[21] your nuptial.

THESEUS.   And we will hear it.

PHILOSTRATE.   No, my noble lord,
It is not for you. I have heard it over,
And it is nothing, nothing in the world;

◄ *What title arrests Theseus's attention? Why does this title have this effect on him?*

◄ *In what way is the play both tedious and brief, according to Philostrate?*

◄ *In what way is the play both tragical and merry?*

◄ *In what way does Philostrate describe Bottom and his companions? How would you characterize Philostrate's attitude?*

◄ *According to Philostrate, what is the only reason anyone would wish to see this play?*

---

17. **The riot . . . rage.** Female followers of Bacchus, god of wine and revelry, supposedly tore apart the great singer Orpheus.
18. **sorting with.** Suitable for
19. **fitted.** In a suitable role
20. **unbreathed.** Inexperienced and untried
21. **against.** In preparation for

Words For Everyday Use	**te • di • ous** (tē ́dē əs) *adj.,* long and tiresome **apt** (apt) *adj.,* suited to its purpose

Unless you can find sport in their intents,
80 Extremely stretch'd, and conn'd[22] with cruel pain,
To do you service.

▶ Why does Theseus
wish to see this
particular play?

THESEUS.   I will hear that play;
For never any thing can be amiss,
When simpleness and duty tender it.
Go bring them in; and take your places, ladies.

Exit PHILOSTRATE.

▶ Why doesn't
Hippolyta wish to see
this particular play?

85 HIPPOLYTA. I love not to see wretchedness o'ercharged,[23]
And duty in his[24] service perishing.

THESEUS. Why, gentle sweet, you shall see no such thing.

HIPPOLYTA. He says they can do nothing in this kind.

THESEUS. The kinder we, to give them thanks for
          nothing.
90 Our sport shall be to take what they mistake
And what poor duty cannot do, noble respect
Takes it in might, not merit.[25]
Where I have come, great clerks[26] have purposed
To greet me with premeditated welcomes;
95 Where I have seen them shiver and look pale,
Make periods in the midst of sentences,
Throttle their practic'd accent in their fears,
And in conclusion dumbly have broke off,
Not paying me a welcome. Trust me, sweet,

▶ What qualities
does Theseus value
most in his subjects?

100 Out of this silence yet I pick'd a welcome;
And in the modesty of fearful duty
I read as much as from the rattling tongue
Of <u>saucy</u> and <u>audacious</u> eloquence.
Love, therefore, and tongue-tied simplicity
105 In least speak most, to my capacity.[27]

Enter PHILOSTRATE.

---

22. **conn'd.** Learned
23. **wretchedness o'ercharged.** Wretched people overburdened or strained
24. **his.** its
25. **Takes it in might, not merit.** Considers the effort of the performers, not only the worth of the performance
26. **clerks.** Scholars
27. **to my capacity.** To my mind; in my opinion

Words
For
Everyday
Use

sauc • y (sô′sē) *adj.,* impudent; pert
au • da • cious (ô dā′shəs) *adj.,* rudely bold

PHILOSTRATE.   So please your Grace, the Prologue is
   address'd.[28]

THESEUS.   Let him approach.   *Flourish trumpet.*

Enter QUINCE *for the Prologue.*

PROLOGUE.   If we offend, it is with our good will.
   That you should think, we come not to offend,
110   But with good will. To show our simple skill,
   That is the true beginning of our end.
   Consider then, we come but in despite.[29]
   We do not come, as minding to content you,
   Our true intent is. All for your delight
115   We are not here. That you should here repent you,
   The actors are at hand; and, by their show,
   You shall know all, that you are like to know.

THESEUS.   This fellow doth not stand upon points.[30]

LYSANDER.   He hath rid his prologue like a rough colt;
120   he knows not the stop.[31] A good moral, my lord: it is
   not enough to speak, but to speak true.

HIPPOLYTA.   Indeed he hath play'd on this prologue like
   a child on a recorder[32]—a sound, but not in government.[33]

THESEUS.   His speech was like a tangled chain;
125   nothing impair'd,[34] but all disorder'd. Who is next?

Enter with a Trumpet before them PYRAMUS *and*
THISBY *and* WALL *and* MOONSHINE *and* LION.

PROLOGUE.   Gentles, perchance you wonder at this show;
   But wonder on till truth make all things plain.
   This man is Pyramus, if you would know;
   This beauteous lady Thisby is certain.
130   This man, with lime and rough-cast, doth present
   Wall, that vile Wall, which did these lovers sunder;[35]
   And through Wall's chink, poor souls, they are content
   To whisper. At the which let no man wonder.
   This man with lantern, dog, and bush of thorn,
135   Presenteth Moonshine; for if you will know,
   By moonshine did these lovers think no scorn[36]
   To meet at Ninus' tomb, there, there to woo.

◄ *What gives this
speech its unintended
meaning?*

◄ *What criticisms
do the nobles have
of the prologue?*

---

28. **Prologue . . . address'd.** Person who delivers the prologue is ready
29. **despite.** Insult, malice
30. **stand upon points.** Punctuate his sentences correctly; worry about details
31. **stop.** Period, endmark of a sentence; also a term for stopping a horse
32. **recorder.** Flute-like musical instrument
33. **government.** Regulation; control
34. **nothing impair'd.** Not broken
35. **sunder.** Keep apart
36. **think no scorn.** Were not ashamed

▶ How did Pyramus and Thisby meet their tragic ends?

This grisly beast, which Lion hight[37] by name,
The trusty Thisby, coming first by night,
140 Did scare away, or rather did affright;
And as she fled her mantle she did fall,[38]
Which Lion vile with bloody mouth did stain.
Anon comes Pyramus, sweet youth and tall,[39]
And finds his trusty Thisby's mantle slain;
145 Whereat, with blade, with bloody blameful blade,
He bravely broach'd[40] his boiling bloody breast;
And Thisby, tarrying in mulberry shade,
His dagger drew, and died. For all the rest,
Let Lion, Moonshine, Wall, and lovers twain[41]
150 At large[42] discourse, while here they do remain.

Exit with PYRAMUS, THISBY, LION *and* MOONSHINE.

THESEUS. I wonder if the lion be to speak.

▶ What is Demetrius's opinion of the actors?

DEMETRIUS. No wonder, my lord; one lion may, when many asses do.

WALL. In this same enterlude[43] it doth befall
155 That I, one Snout by name, present a wall;
And such a wall, as I would have you think,
That had in it a crannied hole or chink,
Through which the lovers, Pyramus and Thisby,
Did whisper often, very secretly.
160 This loam,[44] this rough-cast, and this stone doth show
That I am that same wall, the truth is so
And this the cranny is, right and sinister,[45]
Through which the fearful lovers are to whisper.

THESEUS. Would you desire lime and hair to speak
165 better?

DEMETRIUS. It is the wittiest partition that ever I heard discourse, my lord.

Enter PYRAMUS.

---

37. **hight.** Is called
38. **mantle . . . fall.** She let fall her cloak
39. **tall.** Handsome; brave
40. **broach'd.** Made a hole in
41. **twain.** Two
42. **At large.** At length
43. **enterlude.** Interlude, short play
44. **loam.** Mixture of moistened clay, sand, and straw, used in plastering
45. **sinister.** Left; Snout is saying that the cranny in the wall runs horizontally.

Words For Everyday Use
dis • course (dis´ kôrs´) *vi.,* carry on conversation

THESEUS.   Pyramus draws near the wall. Silence!

PYRAMUS.   O grim-look'd night! O night with hue so black!
170   O night, which ever art when day is not!
O night, O night! alack, alack, alack,
I fear my Thisby's promise is forgot!
And thou, O wall, O sweet, O lovely wall,
That stand'st between her father's ground and mine!
180   Thou wall, O wall, O sweet and lovely wall,
Show me thy chink, to blink through with mine eyne!

                      WALL *holds up his fingers.*

Thanks, courteous wall; Jove shield thee well for this!
But what see I? No Thisby do I see.
O wicked wall, through whom I see no bliss!
185   Curs'd be thy stones for thus deceiving me!

THESEUS.   The wall methinks, being sensible,[46] should
curse again.[47]

◄ *What happens
when Theseus
interrupts the play?*

PYRAMUS.   No, in truth, sir, he should not. "Deceiving
me" is Thisby's cue. She is to enter now, and I am to spy
190   her through the wall. You shall see it will fall pat[48] as I
told you. Yonder she comes.

Enter THISBY.

THISBY.   O wall, full often hast thou heard my moans,
For parting my fair Pyramus and me!
My cherry lips have often kiss'd thy stones,
195   Thy stones with lime and hair knit up in thee.

PYRAMUS.   I see a voice! Now will I to the chink,
To spy and I can hear my Thisby's face.
Thisby!

◄ *What does
Pyramus claim he
can see? What does
he say he can hear?*

THISBY.   My love thou art, my love I think.

200   PYRAMUS.   Think what thou wilt, I am thy lover's grace;[49]
And, like Limander, am I trusty still.

THISBY.   And, like Helen,[50] till the Fates me kill.

PYRAMUS.   Not Shafalus to Procrus[51] was so true.

---

46. **sensible.** Emotionally and intellectually aware
47. **again.** In return to Pyramus's curses
48. **fall pat.** Happen precisely
49. **lover's grace.** Gracious lover
50. **Limander . . . Helen.** Bottom and Flute mean *Leander* and *Hero*, two tragic
lovers from Greek legend. Leander swam to visit Hero each night, guided by the
light in her tower. One night during a storm, the light went out and Leander
drowned. Hero then discovered his body and drowned herself as well.
51. **Shafalus . . . Procrus.** Bottom and Flute mean *Cephalus* and *Procris.*
According to legend, Cephalus was a great hunter who had been beloved by the
goddess Aurora. Later he married Procris, who began to suspect that her husband
was unfaithful because of his frequent hunting trips. Finally, she decided to follow
Cephalus to spy upon him. When Procris emerged from the greenery, Cephalus
mistook her for his prey and shot and killed her with one of his arrows.

THISBY. As Shafalus to Procrus, I to you.

205 **PYRAMUS.** O, kiss me through the hole of this vild[52] wall!

THISBY. I kiss the wall's hole, not your lips at all.

PYRAMUS. Wilt thou at Ninny's tomb meet me straightway?

THISBY. 'Tide[53] life, 'tide death, I come without delay.

Exeunt PYRAMUS *and* THISBY.

WALL. Thus have I, Wall, my part discharged so;
210 And being done, thus Wall away doth go. *Exit.*

THESEUS. Now is the moon used between the two neighbors.

DEMETRIUS. No remedy, my lord, when walls are so willful to hear without warning.[54]

215 **HIPPOLYTA.** This is the silliest stuff that ever I heard.

► *What defense of the play does Theseus offer?*

THESEUS. The best in this kind[55] are but shadows; and the worst are no worse, if imagination <u>amend</u> them.

HIPPOLYTA. It must be your imagination then, and not theirs.

220 **THESEUS.** If we imagine no worse of them than they of themselves, they may pass for excellent men. Here come two noble beasts in, a man and a lion.

Enter LION *and* MOONSHINE.

LION. You, ladies, you, whose gentle hearts do fear
The smallest monstrous mouse that creeps on floor,
225 May now, perchance, both quake and tremble here,
When lion rough in wildest rage doth roar.
Then know that I as Snug the joiner am
A lion fell,[56] nor else no lion's dam,[57]
For, if I should, as lion, come in <u>strife</u>
230 Into this place, 'twere pity on my life.[58]

---

52. **vild.** Vile
53. **'Tide.** Betide, befall, happen, come
54. **walls . . . warning.** Walls are so eager to hear; Demetrius is alluding to the proverb about walls having ears.
55. **kind.** Refers to either plays or actors
56. **fell.** Fierce; also means "hide or skin," referring to Snug's costume
57. **dam.** Mother; lioness
58. **'twere . . . life.** My life would be in jeopardy.

THESEUS. A very gentle[59] beast, and of a good conscience.

DEMETRIUS. The very best at a beast, my lord, that e'er I saw.

235 LYSANDER. This lion is a very fox for his valor.[60]

THESEUS. True; and a goose for his <u>discretion</u>.[61]

DEMETRIUS. Not so, my lord; for his valor cannot carry his discretion, and the fox carries the goose.

THESEUS. His discretion, I am sure, cannot carry his
240 valor; for the goose carries not the fox. It is well; leave it to his discretion, and let us listen to the Moon.

MOON. This lanthorn[62] doth the horned moon
    present—

DEMETRIUS. He should have worn the horns on his head.[63]

245 THESEUS. He is no crescent, and his horns are invisible within the circumference.

MOON. This lanthorn doth the horned moon present;
Myself the man i' th' moon do seem to be.

THESEUS. This is the greatest error of all the rest.
250 The man should be put into the lanthorn. How is it else the man i' th' moon?

DEMETRIUS. He dares not come there for the candle; for, you see, it is already in snuff.[64]

HIPPOLYTA. I am a-weary of this moon. Would he
255 would change!

THESEUS. It appears, by his small light of discretion, that he is in the <u>wane</u>; but yet in courtesy, in all reason, we must stay[65] the time.

◄ *What does the
actor who plays the
moon have to do
when Theseus and
Demetrius interrupt
him?*

---

59. **gentle.** Courteous, polite
60. **very . . . valor.** More clever than brave
61. **a goose . . . discretion.** More silly than sensible
62. **lanthorn.** Lantern; lanterns often had sides made of transparent horn.
63. **horns . . . head.** Demetrius is jesting about cuckolds, or men whose wives have been unfaithful. Cuckolds were commonly represented as wearing two horns on their heads.
64. **in snuff.** In need of being snuffed, or of having the charred end of the candle wick trimmed
65. **stay.** Await

Words
For
Everyday
Use

dis • cre • tion (di skresh´ən) *n.*, prudence

wane (wān) *n.*, gradual decrease of the visible face of
the moon after it has become full

▶ *What does Lysander finally ask the actor to do? What does the moon have to say?*

260   **LYSANDER.**   Proceed, Moon.

MOON.   All that I have to say is to tell you that the lanthorn is the moon, I the man i' th' moon, this thorn-bush my thorn-bush, and this dog my dog.

DEMETRIUS.   Why, all these should be in the lanthorn; 265   for all these are in the moon. But silence! here comes Thisby.

Enter THISBY.

THISBY.   This is old Ninny's tomb. Where is my love?

LION.   O!   *The* LION *roars.* THISBY *runs off.*

DEMETRIUS.   Well roar'd, Lion.

270   **THESEUS.**   Well run, Thisby.

HIPPOLYTA.   Well shone, Moon. Truly, the moon shines with a good grace.   *The* LION *shakes* THISBY'S *mantle.*

THESEUS.   Well mous'd,[66] Lion.

Enter PYRAMUS.

DEMETRIUS.   And then came Pyramus.   *Exit* LION.

275   **LYSANDER.**   And so the lion vanish'd.

PYRAMUS.   Sweet Moon, I thank thee for thy sunny beams;
I thank thee, Moon, for shining now so bright;
For by thy gracious, golden, glittering gleams,
I trust to take of truest Thisby sight.
265   But stay! O spite!
        But mark, poor knight,
     What dreadful dole[67] is here!
        Eyes, do you see?
        How can it be?
270   O dainty duck! O dear!
        Thy mantle good,
        What, stain'd with blood?
     Approach, ye Furies fell![68]
        O Fates,[69] come, come,
275   Cut thread and thrum,[70]
     Quail,[71] crush, conclude, and quell![72]

---

66. **mous'd.** Shaken, as when a cat shakes a mouse
67. **dole.** Sorrowful sight
68. **Furies fell.** Refers to three terrible female spirits (Alecto, Tisiphone, and Megaera) who punish the doers of unavenged crimes in Greek and Roman mythology
69. **Fates.** In classical mythology, three female spirits who control human destiny by spinning the threads of the lives of human beings, by weaving life's tapestry, and by cutting short human lives
70. **Cut thread and thrum.** End my life
71. **Quail.** Overcome
72. **quell.** Put an end to; kill

THESEUS. This passion, and the death of a dear friend,
would go near to make a man look sad.

HIPPOLYTA. Beshrew[73] my heart, but I pity the man.

◀ According to
Theseus, how mov-
ing is Pyramus's
"passion"?

280 PYRAMUS. O, wherefore, Nature, didst thou lions frame?
Since lion vild hath here deflow'r'd my dear;
Which is—no, no—which was the fairest dame
That liv'd, that lov'd, that lik'd, that look'd with cheer.
   Come, tears, confound,
285   Out, sword, and wound
   The pap[74] of Pyramus;
    Ay, that left pap
    Where heart doth hop.   *Stabs himself.*
   Thus die, thus, thus, thus.
290   Now am I dead,
    Now am I fled;
   My soul is in the sky.
    Tongue, lose thy light,
    Moon, take thy flight,   *Exit* MOONSHINE.[75]
295   Now die, die, die, die, die.   *Dies.*

◀ What does
Pyramus keep doing
even though he says
he is dead?

DEMETRIUS. No die, but an ace,[76] for him; for he is but one.

LYSANDER. Less than an ace, man; for he is dead, he is
nothing.

THESEUS. With the help of a surgeon he might yet
300 recover, and yet prove an ass.

HIPPOLYTA. How chance Moonshine is gone before
Thisby comes back and finds her lover?

Enter THISBY.

THESEUS. She will find him by starlight. Here she comes,
and her passion ends the play.

305 HIPPOLYTA. Methinks she should not use a long one for
such a Pyramus. I hope she will be brief.

DEMETRIUS. A mote will turn[77] the balance, which
Pyramus, which Thisby, is the better: he for a man, God
warr'nt us; she for a woman, God bless us.

310 LYSANDER. She hath spied him already with those sweet
eyes.

---

73. **Beshrew.** Mild oath
74. **pap.** Breast
75. **Moon . . . MOONSHINE.** Moonshine was intended to remain on stage, but
because Pyramus has said *moon* where he meant *tongue* and vice versa, the
character playing moonshine believes that this is his cue to exit.
76. **No . . . ace.** Not a whole die but the side with one spot on a die
77. **A . . . turn.** A very small thing will determine

DEMETRIUS. And thus she means, *videlicet*—[78]

THISBY.   Asleep, my love?
        What, dead, my dove?
315   O Pyramus, arise!
         Speak, speak! Quite dumb?
         Dead, dead? A tomb
      Must cover thy sweet eyes.
        These lily lips,
320   This cherry nose,
      These yellow cowslip cheeks,
        Are gone, are gone!
        Lovers, make moan;
      His eyes were green as leeks.[79]
325   O Sisters Three,[80]
        Come, come to me,
      With hands as pale as milk;
        Lay them in <u>gore</u>,
        Since you have shore[81]
330   With shears his thread of silk.
        Tongue, not a word!
        Come, trusty sword,
      Come, blade, my breast <u>imbrue</u>!

                           Stabs herself.

      And farewell, friends;
335   Thus Thisby ends;
      Adieu, adieu, adieu.   *Dies.*

THESEUS. Moonshine and Lion are left to bury the dead.

DEMETRIUS. Ay, and Wall too.

BOTTOM. [*Starting up.*] No, I assure you, the wall is
340 down that parted their fathers. Will it please you to see
the epilogue, or to hear[82] a Bergomask dance[83] between
two of our company?

▶ What does
Bottom do when the
nobles discuss
whether the wall will
help to bury Pyramus
and Thisby? Why is
this unusual?

---

78. **means, *videlicet*.** Laments as follows
79. **leeks.** Onionlike vegetables
80. **Sisters Three.** The Fates
81. **shore.** Shorn, cut short
82. **see . . . hear.** Another of Bottom's common blunders; the order of *see* and
hear should be reversed.
83. **Bergomask dance.** Rustic dance

**Words
For
Everyday
Use**

gore (gôr) *n.,* blood shed from a wound
im • brue (im broo´) *vt.,* wet, soak, or stain, especially
with blood

THESEUS. No epilogue, I pray you; for your play needs
no excuse. Never excuse; for when the players are all
345 dead, there need none to be blam'd. Marry, if he that
writ it had play'd Pyramus, and hang'd himself in
Thisby's garter, it would have been a fine tragedy; and
so it is, truly, and very notably discharg'd. But come,
your Bergomask; let your epilogue alone.   *A dance.*
350 The iron tongue of midnight hath told[84] twelve.
Lovers, to bed, 'tis almost fairy time.
I fear we shall outsleep the coming morn
As much as we this night have overwatch'd.[85]
This palpable-gross[86] play hath well <u>beguil'd</u>
355 The heavy <u>gait</u> of night. Sweet friends, to bed.
A fortnight hold we this solemnity
In nightly revels and new jollity.   *Exeunt.*

Enter PUCK.

PUCK.   Now the hungry lion roars,
                    And the wolf behowls the moon
360   Whilst the heavy ploughman snores,
                    All with weary task foredone.[87]
                    Now the wasted brands[88] do glow,
                    Whilst the screech-owl, screeching loud,
                    Puts the wretch that lies in woe
365   In remembrance of a shroud.[89]
                    Now it is the time of night
                    That the graves, all gaping wide,
                    Every one lets forth his sprite,[90]
                    In the church-way paths to glide.
370   And we fairies, that do run
                    By the triple Hecat's[91] team
                    From the presence of the sun,
                    Following darkness like a dream,

◄ *What time is it?
What time is
approaching?*

---

84. **told.** Struck
85. **overwatch'd.** Seen too much of; stayed up too late
86. **palpable-gross.** Obviously coarse
87. **foredone.** Tired out
88. **wasted brands.** Burnt logs
89. **shroud.** Cloth used to wrap a corpse for burial
90. **his sprite.** Its ghost
91. **triple Hecat's.** Refers to Hecate's three roles as goddess of the moon, the
earth, and the underworld of the dead

Words
For
Everyday
Use
be • guile (bē gīl´) *vt.*, pass time pleasantly
gait (gāt) *n.*, manner of moving on foot

▶ Why has Puck been sent to this place?

375 Now are frolic.[92] Not a mouse
Shall disturb this hallowed house.
I am sent with broom before,
To sweep the dust behind the door.[93]

Enter King and Queen of Fairies (OBERON and TITANIA) with all their TRAIN.

OBERON. Through the house give glimmering light
By the dead and drowsy fire,
380 Every elf and fairy sprite
Hop as light as bird from brier,
And this ditty,[94] after me,
Sing, and dance it <u>trippingly</u>.
First, rehearse your song by rote,
385 To each word a warbling note.
Hand in hand, with fairy grace,
Will we sing, and bless this place.

Song and dance.

▶ Why have Oberon, Titania, and their fairy followers come to this place?

OBERON. Now, until the break of day
Through this house each fairy stray.
390 To the best bride-bed will we,
Which by us shall blessed be;
And the issue, there create,[95]
Ever shall be fortunate.
So shall all the couples three
395 Ever true in loving be;
And the blots of Nature's hand
Shall not in their issue stand;
Never mole, hare-lip, nor scar,
Nor mark prodigious,[96] such as are
400 Despised in nativity,
Shall upon their children be.
With this field-dew consecrate,
Every fairy take his gait,
And each several chamber bless

▶ What blessing do the fairies offer the newly married couples?

---

92. **frolic.** Frolicsome, jolly
93. **To . . . door.** Shakespeare's contemporaries believed that Puck, or Robin Goodfellow, was a domestic spirit who sometimes helped with everyday chores.
94. **ditty.** Short, simple song
95. **issue . . . create.** Children created there
96. **mark prodigious.** Birthmark

Words For Everyday Use

trip • ping • ly (trip´iŋ lē) *adv.*, lightly and quickly; nimbly

405		Through this palace, with sweet peace,
		And the owner of it blest
		Ever shall in safety rest.
		Trip away; make no stay;
		Meet me all by break of day.

Exeunt OBERON, TITANIA, *and* TRAIN.

410	PUCK.	If we shadows have offended,
		Think but this, and all is mended,
		That you have but slumb'red here
		While these visions did appear.
		And this weak and idle theme
415		No more yielding but[97] a dream,
		Gentles, do not reprehend.
		If you pardon, we will mend.
		And, as I am an honest Puck,
		If we have unearned luck
420		Now to scape the serpent's tongue,[98]
		We will make amends ere long;
		Else the Puck a liar call.
		So, good night unto you all.
		Give me your hands,[99] if we be friends
425		And Robin shall restore amends.	*Exit.*

◄ *According to Puck, if you did not enjoy this play, how should you think of it?*

---

97. **but.** Then
98. **serpent's tongue.** Hissing of the audience
99. **Give . . . hands.** Applaud, clap

Responding to the Selection

What was your opinion of the artisans' play? Do you share the assessment of the aristocratic audience who viewed it, or do you have some other opinion? What do you think about how the audience behaved when viewing the play? If you were in their position, would you behave in the same way, or differently?

Reviewing the Selection

Recalling and Interpreting

1. **R:** What is Theseus's opinion of Hermia and Lysander's and Helena and Demetrius's story? What does the audience know that Theseus does not? According to Theseus, by what are lunatics, lovers, and poets misled? In what way are these three classes of people similar? What is Hippolyta's opinion of the story told by the four young Athenians?

2. **I:** Explain whether you think Theseus's opinion befits his experiences and his position. What evidence contradicts Theseus's opinion? Based on the play's events, whose opinion of lunatics, lovers, and poets do you think Shakespeare shared, Theseus's or Hippolyta's? In other words, what was Shakespeare's view of "cool reason" versus "imagination"?

3. **R:** What warning are the nobles given about the quality of the artisans' play, "A tedious brief scene of young Pyramus / And his love Thisby; very tragical mirth"? What reasons does Theseus give for wishing to see this play anyway? What reasons does Hippolyta give for not wishing to see it?

4. **I:** Whose attitude toward the artisans is more gracious and courteous, Theseus's or Hippolyta's? Explain what Theseus's attitude reveals about him as a ruler. Why might it be important for the audience to form this conception of Theseus's ability to rule toward the end of a comedy?

5. **R:** What is the basic story line of the play that the artisans present? How do the nobles react to the events that occur in this play?

6. **I:** In what way are the story line and subject matter of the play within the play related to what has occurred in *A Midsummer Night's Dream?* Might Lysander, Demetrius, Hermia, and Helena have been more moved by this play in act I than they are in act V? Why do you think they react as they do to this play now that their experiences in the wood are behind them and remembered only as strange dreams?

7. **R:** What does Theseus say about the time just before the nobles retire to bed? When Puck enters, what does he say about the time of night? about this particular house? When Oberon and Titania appear, what blessing do they bestow upon the occupants of the house?

8. **I:** The nobles seem to have forgotten all about the world of the fairies by the play's end. In what way do the fairies assert their importance to human life at the play's end? Why might this blessing be especially significant if *A Midsummer Night's Dream* was written and first performed for a courtly wedding?

Synthesizing

9. Even though Theseus claims he can pick a better welcome from "fearful duty" than from "audacious eloquence," he and the other nobles interrupt the artisans' play with constant comments, critiques, and jests. For example, when Theseus and Demetrius interrupt the character who plays the moon to jest about cuckolds, the moon has to repeat his first line. When the nobles interrupt to exchange witty jests again, the moon actually has to be told to proceed before he will continue. What do you think of the nobles' behavior during the play? What does their behavior reveal about the nobles as characters? Why do the nobles find it irresistible to comment on this play? What have the artisans misunderstood about the theater? In what way have the artisans affected their play by removing all dramatic illusion and realism? In a play, what must take precedence—cool reason or imagination?

10. In the Pyramus and Thisby play, in what way does Bottom violate one of the conventions of theater—the distance between actor and audience? Explain how Bottom forces the nobles from their roles as observing audience members to make them more closely involved with the play. In what way do Bottom's actions point out that not only Pyramus and Thisby but all the characters in *A Midsummer Night's Dream* are mere "shadows," or actors? Explain whether the nobles are aware of their own roles as actors in this play. In what way does this lifting of the illusions of literature and the theater affect your perceptions of the play? Explain whether it reminds you that the whole play is, after all, just a play.

Understanding Literature

1. Verbal Irony. In **verbal irony** a statement is made that implies its opposite. The artisans begin their play with a prologue delivered by Quince. Quince punctuates this prologue so poorly that it becomes an example of verbal irony—Quince says the opposite of what he means to say. Find a couple of examples of verbal irony in this passage. Explain what Quince means to say to his audience and what he in effect says.

2. Parody and Satire. A **parody** is a literary work that imitates another work for humorous, often satirical purposes. **Satire** is humorous writing or speech intended to point out errors, falsehoods, foibles, or failings. Through the device of the artisans' production of *Pyramus and Thisby,* Shakespeare parodies and satirizes a form of drama immensely popular in the years before *A Midsummer Night's Dream* was written—Senecan tragedy, or tragedy modeled after the plays of the ancient Roman tragedian Seneca. Characteristics of English Senecan tragedy were melodrama, or overblown expressions of emotion that are not warranted given the lack of character development, and the use of stereotypical phrases to express grief, like addresses to the Fates and Furies or direct, overblown addresses to something or someone (O night! O death! O love!). Shakespeare also parodies bad poetry: poor rhymes; trite and clichéd similes and metaphors (such as the comparisons between human features and flowers); and overuse of alliteration, or the repetition of initial consonant sounds. Find examples of lines in the Pyramus and Thisby play where Shakespeare is clearly parodying and satirizing Senecan tragedy and bad poetry. At what is he poking fun in these lines? Explain why Shakespeare may have chosen to parody these things in his play. Of what must he have been confident?

3. Aim. A writer's **aim** is the primary purpose that his or her work is meant to achieve. What is the aim of the final speech of the play? In what way does Puck continue Bottom's work in lifting the illusion of the theater for the audience?

Plot Analysis of *A Midsummer Night's Dream*

The following diagram, known as Freytag's Pyramid, illustrates the main plot of *A Midsummer Night's Dream*. For definitions and more information on the parts of a plot, see the Handbook of Literary Terms.

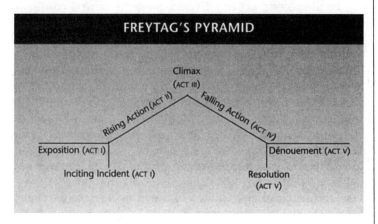

FREYTAG'S PYRAMID

Climax (ACT III)

Rising Action (ACT II)

Falling Action (ACT IV)

Exposition (ACT I)

Inciting Incident (ACT I)

Dénouement (ACT V)

Resolution (ACT V)

Exposition and Inciting Incident (Act I)

In a five-act play, the first act typically presents the setting and the main characters. The central conflict is also developed. In *A Midsummer Night's Dream*, Athens is introduced and the wood in which much of the action of the story will take place is mentioned. The reader or audience meets Theseus, ruler of Athens, and Hippolyta, queen of the Amazons, whom Theseus will wed in four days. Egeus, a nobleman, approaches Theseus accompanied by his daughter Hermia and two young men named Lysander and Demetrius. Egeus introduces the story's central conflict: both Lysander and Demetrius love Hermia. Hermia loves Lysander in return, but Egeus wishes his daughter to marry Demetrius. Egeus demands that Hermia be killed or sent to a convent, as the law dictates, should she refuse to obey her father. To escape this harsh Athenian law, Lysander and Hermia plan to meet in a wood outside Athens and flee to an aunt's house where they can be wed. The two inform Helena, a friend of Hermia's, of their plan. Helena, however, is desperately in love with Demetrius, who once swore love to her but now scorns her for Hermia. Helena vows to inform Demetrius of Hermia and Lysander's plan to escape. The reader or audience is also introduced to a group of artisans—Quince, Bottom, Snug, Flute, Snout, and Starveling—who plan to perform a dramatization of the Pyramus and Thisby story to celebrate Theseus and Hippolyta's wedding; they arrange to meet for rehearsal in the wood outside Athens the following night.

Rising Action (Act II)

In the second act of a five-act play, the central conflict is developed. In act II of *A Midsummer Night's Dream*, the reader or audience is introduced to a conflict between Oberon and Titania, king and queen of the fairies. Oberon wishes Titania to give him a small Indian boy she has in her charge, but she refuses because the boy is the son of a former friend who died in childbirth. Oberon asks his loyal fairy servant Puck to find him a special flower, the juice of which, placed in a sleeping person's eyes, has the power to make that person fall in love with the first creature he or she sees on awakening. Oberon plans to use this flower on Titania as part of a plan to obtain the boy from her. Oberon then observes Demetrius, who has followed Hermia into the wood, as he rejects Helena who faithfully follows him. Oberon tells Puck to put some of the magic juice in the scornful Athenian youth's eyes. While Oberon anoints Titania's eyes, Puck blunders and administers the potion to Lysander rather than to Demetrius. Helena, who has been abandoned by Demetrius, awakens Lysander who immediately falls in love with and follows her, forgetting his former affection for Hermia.

Climax (Act III)

The third act of a five-act play presents a decisive occurrence that determines the future course of events in the play. In act III of *A Midsummer Night's Dream*, the artisans rehearse their play as an amused Puck observes. Puck transforms Bottom, giving him an ass's head, and Bottom's strange appearance startles his companions so that they all run away. Bottom then awakens the sleeping Titania, who, under the influence of the juice of the flower, immediately falls in love with him. Meanwhile, Oberon and Puck try to correct their mistake, so they anoint Demetrius's eyes and bring Helena and Lysander to where Demetrius lies sleeping. Demetrius awakes, also falls in love with Helena, and argues with Lysander about who deserves Helena's affections. Hermia, upset that Lysander has abandoned her, enters the scene to hear Lysander declare that he hates her and loves Helena. Helena, meanwhile, is convinced that all three have joined together to mock her. Helena and Hermia fight, and Demetrius and Lysander go off to duel for Helena's love. Oberon orders Puck, who is delighted with all the mayhem he has caused, to separate Demetrius and Lysander and keep them from fighting and to anoint Lysander's eyes with an herb that will remove his charmed love for Helena and restore his love for Hermia. Puck manages to lead the men away from each other until they grow frustrated with their search and sleep. Puck then places the remedy on Lysander's eyes.

Falling Action (Act IV)

The fourth act of a five-act play presents events that happen as a result of the climax, or crisis. In act IV, Oberon removes the charm from Titania's eyes now that he has obtained the changeling boy from her, and Puck removes the spell that gave Bottom an ass's head. Thus, an end comes to the conflict between Titania and Oberon. The fairies put a charmed sleep upon Demetrius, Helena, Hermia, Lysander, and Bottom, so that the five will believe their experiences in the wood are dreams. As Theseus, Hippolyta, Egeus, and other nobles go out hunting, they encounter the missing Athenians. Once Theseus learns that Demetrius no longer wishes to marry Hermia and loves Helena, Theseus declares that the two happy couples shall be wed alongside him and Hippolyta. Meanwhile, the artisans have been despairing Bottom's absence. After he awakens, Bottom rejoins his companions and tells them that their play is to be performed.

Resolution and Dénouement (Act V)

The fifth act of a five-act play presents the event that resolves, or ends, the central conflict. It also ties up loose ends. In act V of *A Midsummer Night's Dream*, the three newly married couples celebrate their nuptials by watching the artisans' play about Pyramus and Thisby, which proves to be unintentionally comic. After all retire to bed, Puck, Oberon, Titania, and the other fairies come to bless the newly married couples.

Creative Writing Activities

Creative Writing A: Parody

In *A Midsummer Night's Dream*, Shakespeare parodies Senecan tragedy and bad poetry through the device of the artisans' play. The key to any skillful parody is that it must be clear to your audience that you are poking fun at a type or genre of literature rather than producing a bad example of that literature. Thus, parodies are a good exercise in clever and careful writing. Choose a type or genre of literature that you would like to parody. You might even choose a specific literary work or part of a literary work to parody. For example, you might choose to parody twentieth-century confessional poetry, or poetry that describes, sometimes with painful explicitness, the private or personal affairs of the writer, or you might parody something more specific, such as that part of act II of *A Midsummer Night's Dream* in which the fairies are introduced. Remember that you will need to be very familiar with the type of literature or literary work you are parodying. Ask yourself what qualities or literary techniques in this literature might be exaggerated or overdone to humorous effect.

Creative Writing B: Epilogue

An epilogue is a concluding section or statement, often one that comments on or draws conclusions about the work as a whole. Shakespeare ended many of his plays with a form of epilogue—often a lone character will remain on stage to either explain something to the audience or to appeal to the audience for applause. Think of a play or other literary work you have enjoyed and write an epilogue for it, appealing to an audience for applause. (Note: If you choose a nondramatic work, you should imagine that this work has been adapted for the stage.) Think about which of the characters from the work would be most appropriate to deliver such an epilogue. Examine this character's dialogue and think about his or her personal qualities to explore how the character might appeal to an audience for applause.

Creative Writing C: Soliloquy

A soliloquy is a speech delivered by a lone character that reveals the speaker's thoughts and feelings. An example of a soliloquy appears at the very end of act I, scene i. Helena is alone on stage and reveals her feelings about Demetrius and her plan to tell him of Lysander and Hermia's scheme. Soliloquies are particularly important in dramas because there is no narration to tell what the characters' inner feelings are; everything must be revealed through action and dialogue, so soliloquies are one way dramatists allow the audience to better glimpse a character's feelings and motivations.

As you have discovered, one of the important themes in *A Midsummer Night's Dream* is the distinction between theater and everyday life. Imagine that you are a character in a play and that your life and the lives of the people close to you is the subject of this play. Think about some recent decisions you have made, or how you feel about a current relationship. After you have freewritten your thoughts about some current issue in your life, write yourself a soliloquy, revealing your motivations, thoughts, and feelings about this issue or event. While you might try experimenting with iambic pentameter, the meter in which many of Shakespeare's soliloquies are written, you can also write your soliloquy in prose, as long as your language is vivid and revealing.

Creative Writing D: Dialogue

Dialogue is conversation involving two or more people or characters. Plays are made up of dialogue and stage directions. One of the most humorous scenes in *A Midsummer Night's Dream*—at least for the audience and for Puck who is observing—occurs in act III, when the four young Athenians confront each other with their feelings of love, jealousy, and suspicion. Write your own dialogue which involves a confrontation among young people who have some romantic conflicts. You might write an argument between a young couple, or you might write dialogue for characters involved in a love triangle as Shakespeare has done. Before you begin writing your dialogue, freewrite about your characters and their possible relationships and feelings toward each other. Try to make your dialogue as realistic as possible; your reader should be able to imagine the words actually being spoken.

Critical Writing Activities

The following topics are suitable for short critical essays on *A Midsummer Night's Dream*. An essay written on one of these topics should begin with an introductory paragraph that states the thesis, or main idea, of the essay. The introductory paragraph should be followed by several paragraphs that support the thesis using evidence from the drama. The essay should conclude with a paragraph that summarizes the points made in the essay and that resolves the thesis.

Critical Writing Activity A: Analyzing Theme

A theme is a central idea in a literary work. Shakespeare develops many themes in *A Midsummer Night's Dream*. Choose one of the themes listed below, and write an essay in which you analyze Shakespeare's treatment of this theme and trace its development throughout the drama.
• Love and Marriage
• Friendship
• Family
• Dreams versus Reality
• Imagination versus Reason
• Chaos versus Order
• Growing up
If you prefer, you might choose more than one theme and explain the way in which these themes are related. To begin, freewrite your thoughts about this theme or themes. Then, skim through *A Midsummer Night's Dream*, making a list of passages in which this theme or themes are treated. After reviewing these passages and your freewriting, develop a thesis about your chosen theme or themes; support your thesis in following paragraphs, using examples and quotations from the passages you listed; and come to a conclusion in a final paragraph.

Critical Writing Activity B: Comedy and Tragedy

As you have read in the section "*A Midsummer Night's Dream* in Context," on page xv, Shakespeare wrote this play at the same time he was writing *The Tragedy of Romeo and Juliet*. This tragedy is similar to *A Midsummer Night's Dream* in that two young lovers are separated because of their families, and the lovers meet secretly despite their parents' wishes. While this situation leads to tragedy in *Romeo and Juliet*, it leads to comedy in *A Midsummer Night's Dream*; however, some have argued that the four lovers, Hermia, Lysander, Demetrius, and Helena only narrowly avert tragedy. Write an essay in which you explain what elements in *A Midsummer Night's Dream* are potentially tragic, as well as how tragedy is averted. You should also explain what view of tragic couples is portrayed in *A Midsummer Night's Dream*, particularly in the treatment of the Pyramus and Thisby story. While you do not have to be familiar with *The Tragedy of Romeo and Juliet* to write this essay, if you are familiar with it you may wish to compare and contrast the two works to show where and how the story lines diverge. You might also wish to read Ovid's version of the story of Pyramus and Thisbe, included in Selections for Additional Reading on page 99.

Critical Writing Activity C: The Theater in *A Midsummer Night's Dream*

Much of *A Midsummer Night's Dream* focuses on actors, acting, and theatrical illusions, and the play features a play within a play. Write an essay in which you explain the view of the theater presented in *A Midsummer Night's Dream*. What does Shakespeare indicate about realism, illusion, and imagination in the theater? What makes for a bad play and what makes for a good play? Finally, in what ways does Shakespeare seem to indicate that theater is similar to and different from the everyday world? How can one tell the difference between the two? To write this essay, you should review the play carefully, focusing on passages that deal with actors and acting and looking carefully at the fifth act in which the play within the play is presented.

Critical Writing Activity D: Analyzing Characters

A Midsummer Night's Dream presents characters who have awed, delighted, and amused audiences for centuries. Choose one of the characters you find most interesting and analyze that character's role in the story. Possible topics to consider include the following:
- Bottom's role: Is Bottom a mere clown, or is he an archetypal wise fool—a character who speaks more truly than he knows, even if to humorous effect? How do his companions perceive him? How do the nobles perceive him? How does Bottom perceive himself? How does he react to new situations? Why is he the only character to interact directly with the fairies? What is significant about the way in which he enacts the part of Pyramus? What does Bottom point out to other characters and the audience about theater? about themselves?

- Oberon and Titania's role: In what way do events in these characters' lives seem to directly affect both humans and the natural world? Given that these characters have so much supernatural and magical power, do they use this power wisely? Why do they occasionally blunder? In what ways are they similar to or different from humans?
- Puck's role: What events in the story does Puck make possible? How does he feel about humans? Does he ever feel pity for them? What seems to motivate Puck as a character? Why is he the character chosen to close the play? What do his final speeches reveal about him?
- Theseus and Hippolyta's role: How would you describe Theseus as a ruler? What are his good qualities and his bad qualities? How would you characterize Theseus and Hippolyta's relationship? What do their differing views about the truth of the young lovers' story and about the artisans' play reveal about them?
- Egeus's role: How would you describe Egeus as a father? Why are his plans foiled in the end? Why isn't Egeus heard from again once Theseus decides Lysander will wed Hermia and Demetrius will wed Helena? How do you think Shakespeare viewed fathers who meddle in their children's relationships?
- Helena, Hermia, Demetrius, and Lysander's role: Explore these four characters as a group. In what ways are Helena and Hermia similar? different? In what ways are Demetrius and Lysander similar? different? What happens to the identities of these characters in the wood outside Athens? In what way is their story a story about growing up?

After you have chosen a character or group of characters you would like to explore, freewrite your ideas, using the appropriate set of questions above as a guide. Then review the text of *A Midsummer Night's Dream* carefully, focusing on passages that reveal something about your chosen character(s). Use this information to help develop and support your thesis about the significance of this character(s) in *A Midsummer Night's Dream*.

Projects

Project A: Representing *A Midsummer Night's Dream* in Art

Choose a favorite moment, character(s), or setting from *A Midsummer Night's Dream* and represent your chosen subject in a sketch, painting, collage, sculpture, or model. For example, you might represent the fairies' wood outside Athens in a collage, using dried or fabric flowers and leaves and images of fairies set on a background of star-filled skies; you might create a painting of Bottom with an ass's head, Puck with his broom, or Titania sleeping in her bower; you might create a model depicting the artisans' production of the Pyramus and Thisby story as the nobles watch on one side of the stage. You may wish to research what typical Renaissance sets or costumes looked like before you begin your artistic representation, or you may wish to rely on your imagination alone.

Project B: Enacting *A Midsummer Night's Dream*

Today, *A Midsummer Night's Dream* is one of Shakespeare's most frequently performed plays. Work with a group of your classmates to rehearse and enact a brief scene from *A Midsummer Night's Dream*. After your group has chosen a scene that everyone likes, choose a director and a stage manager, and assign acting roles to the rest of the group members. The director will coach actors on their movement and the delivery of their lines. The stage manager will plan rehearsal times, prepare scripts, prompt actors with their lines, and generally help the director. If your group has too few actors for the scene that you have chosen, do what Shakespeare did and have actors with smaller parts play more than one role. Each group should rehearse their scene several times before delivering it to the rest of the class.

If you prefer, you might even work together as a class on an extended project to enact the whole of the play. To begin, you should divide up the many tasks necessary to put on a play; in addition to a director and a stage manager, you will need people to design and help construct a set, a costume designer, a properties manager, and a person to manage lighting and sound effects. If your whole class decides to put on a performance of *A Midsummer Night's Dream*, you might invite students from other classes, friends, and family members to your performance.

Project C: Researching Famous Romantic Couples

A major theme in *A Midsummer Night's Dream* is love and romance. Work in small groups to research famous romantic pairs in history, film, or literature. Although you can choose any famous couple to research, possible subjects include Romeo and Juliet, Tristan and Isolde, Lancelot and Guinevere, Paolo and Francesca, Queen Elizabeth and Sir Walter Raleigh, Troilus and Cressida, Antony and Cleopatra, Helen of Troy and Paris, and Odysseus and Penelope. Your group should research this couple's story, focusing on how the two met and fell in love, any obstacles in the way of their love, and whether their love ended happily or in tragedy. You may also wish to find visual representations of the couple to share with the class. Your group should then share the story of your chosen romantic pair with your classmates. After all groups have given their presentations, discuss similarities and differences in the stories. Have you shared more stories about love that ends happily or love that ends tragically? Why might this be? What are some common obstacles that stand in the way of love?

Project D: The Psychology and Science of Love

Considering that Lysander and Demetrius are equal in fortune, rank, and birth, why does Hermia love Lysander, but not Demetrius? Why does Demetrius fall out of love with Helena and in love with Hermia? Why does Helena continue to love Demetrius despite his cruel behavior? Although love is one human emotion that may seem mysterious and inexplicable and, as Theseus notes, seems to have little to do with "cool reason," scientists and psychologists alike have studied the phenomenon of love to determine what makes people prefer one person to another, what makes people fall in love, and what makes some people remain in love even when such feelings are painful or even dangerous. Work in small groups to research the psychology or science of love. Possible sources of information include psychiatric or medical journals. Your group may even wish to interview older couples whose love has lasted many years to ask them how they fell in love and their secrets for a healthy, happy relationship. Your group should narrow your research to exploring one particular field or school of thought, such as pheromone research, behaviorist research, or the results of a particular study conducted by researchers. Each group should report its findings to the class.

Selections for Additional Reading

"The Story of Pyramus and Thisbe"
from *Metamorphoses*
by Ovid

Publius Ovidius Naso (43 BC–AD 17) is better known to many readers as Ovid. He was born in Sulmo, east of Rome, to a well-to-do family that was able to send him to Athens to finish his education. Originally destined for a legal career, he soon turned to poetry and gained some success with a series of love poems, Amores, written around 15 BC. Ovid's early work contained a casual and witty treatment of love and marriage, and it is as a love poet that he was principally known from his own time until the Renaissance. Ovid's fortunes changed drastically in AD 8, when he was banished from Rome by Emperor Augustus for an offense that remains unknown. He was sent to live in Tomis, part of modern-day Romania, then an outpost of the Roman Empire. There Ovid spent the rest of his life, at times depressed and despondent, while his wife vainly pleaded his case back in Rome. Ovid's years in exile were still productive, for he continued to write poetry. His interest in love as a poetic subject decreased, and during this time he wrote Metamorphoses, generally considered to be his greatest work. This work, whose title means "changing forms," is a vast compendium of the myths of classical Greece and Rome, many of which deal with miraculous transformations. This excerpt from Metamorphoses relates the tragic story of young lovers Pyramus and Thisbe.

"Next door to each other, in the brickwalled city
Built by Semiramis, lived a boy and girl,
Pyramus, a most handsome fellow, Thisbe,
Loveliest of all those Eastern girls. Their nearness
Made them acquainted, and love grew, in time,
So that they would have married, but their parents
Forbade it. But their parents could not keep them
From being in love: their nods and gestures showed it—
You know how fire suppressed burns all the fiercer.
There was a chink in the wall between the houses,
A flaw the careless builder had never noticed,
Nor anyone else, for many years, detected,
But the lovers found it—love is a finder, always—
Used it to talk through, and the loving whispers
Went back and forth in safety. They would stand
One on each side, listening for each other,

Happy if each could hear the other's breathing,
And then they would scold the wall: 'You envious barrier,
Why get in our way? Would it be too much to ask you
To open wide for an embrace, or even
Permit us room to kiss in? Still, we are grateful,
We owe you something, we admit; at least
You let us talk together.' But their talking
Was futile, rather; and when evening came
They would say *Goodnight!* and give the goodnight kisses
That never reached the other.
                              "The next morning
Came, and the fires of night burnt out, and sunshine
Dried the night frost, and Pyramus and Thisbe
Met at the usual place, and first, in whispers,
Complained, and came—high time!—to a decision.
That night, when all was quiet, they would fool
Their guardians, or try to, come outdoors,
Run away from home, and even leave the city.
And, not to miss each other, as they wandered
In the wide fields, where should they meet? At Ninus'
Tomb, they supposed, was best; there was a tree there,
A mulberry-tree, loaded with snow-white berries,
Near a cool spring. The plan was good, the daylight
Was very slow in going, but at last
The sun went down into the waves, as always,
And the night rose, as always, from those waters.

And Thisbe opened her door, so sly, so cunning,
There was no creaking of the hinge, and no one
Saw her go through the darkness, and she came,
Veiled, to the tomb of Ninus, sat there waiting
Under the shadow of the mulberry-tree.
Love made her bold. But suddenly, here came something!—
A lioness, her jaws a crimson froth
With the blood of cows, fresh-slain, came there for water,
And far off through the moonlight Thisbe saw her
And ran, all scared, to hide herself in a cave,
And dropped her veil as she ran. The lioness,
Having quenched her thirst, came back to the woods, and saw
The girl's light veiL and mangled it and mouthed it
With bloody jaws. Pyramus, coming there
Too late, saw tracks in the dust, turned pale, and paler
Seeing the bloody veil. 'One night,' he cried,
'Will kill two lovers, and one of them, most surely,
Deserved a longer life. It is all my fault,
I am the murderer, poor girl; I told you

To come here in the night, to all this terror,
And was not here before you, to protect you.
Come, tear my flesh, devour my guilty body,
Come, lions, all of you, whose lairs lie hidden
Under this rock! I am acting like a coward,
Praying for death.' He lifts the veil and takes it
Into the shadow of their tree; he kisses
The veil he knows so well his tears run down
Into its folds: 'Drink my blood too!' he cries,
And draws his sword, and plunges it into his body,
And, dying, draws it out, warm from the wound.
As he lay there on the ground, the spouting blood
Leaped high, just as a pipe sends water spurting
Through a small hissing opening, when broken
With a flaw in the lead, and all the air is sprinkled.
The fruit of the tree, from that red spray, turned crimson,
And the roots, soaked with the blood, dyed all the berries
The same dark hue.
         "Thisbe came out of hiding,
Still frightened, but a little fearful, also,
To disappoint her lover. She kept looking
Not only with her eyes, but all her heart,
Eager to tell him of those terrible dangers,
About her own escape. She recognized
The place, the shape of the tree, but there was something
Strange or peculiar in the berries' color.
Could this be right? And then she saw a quiver
Of limbs on bloody ground, and started backward,
Paler than boxwood, shivering, as water
Stirs when a little breeze ruffles the surface.
It was not long before she knew her lover,
And tore her hair, and beat her innocent bosom
With her little fists, embraced the well-loved body,
Filling the wounds with tears, and kissed the lips
Cold in his dying. 'O my Pyramus,'
She wept, 'What evil fortune takes you from me?
Pyramus, answer me! Your dearest Thisbe
Is calling you. Pyramus, listen! Lift your head!'
He heard the name of Thisbe, and he lifted
His eyes, with the weight of death heavy upon them,
And saw her face, and closed his eyes.
         "And Thisbe
Saw her own veil, and saw the ivory scabbard
With no sword in it, and understood. 'Poor boy,'
She said, 'So, it was your own hand,
Your love, that took your life away. I too

Have a brave hand for this one thing, I too
Have love enough, and this will give me strength
For the last wound. I will follow you in death,
Be called the cause and comrade of your dying.
Death was the only one could keep you from me,
Death shall not keep you from me. Wretched parents
Of Pyramus and Thisbe, listen to us,
Listen to both our prayers, do not begrudge us,
Whom death has joined, lying at last together
In the same tomb. And you, O tree, now shading
The body of one, and very soon to shadow
The bodies of two, keep in remembrance always
The sign of our death, the dark and mournful color.'
She spoke, and fitting the sword-point at her breast,
Fell forward on the blade, still warm and reeking
With her lover's blood. Her prayers touched the gods,
And touched her parents, for the mulberry fruit
Still reddens at its ripeness, and the ashes
Rest in a common urn."

from *The Tragedy of Romeo and Juliet*
by William Shakespeare

In this excerpt from Romeo and Juliet, *Juliet's parents behave much like Hermia's father in* A Midsummer Night's Dream, *trying to force Juliet to marry a man she does not love.*

ACT III, SCENE iv: **Capulet's house.**

Enter old CAPULET, *his* WIFE, *and* PARIS.

CAPULET.   Things have fall'n out, sir, so unluckily
That we have had no time to move our daughter.
Look you, she lov'd her kinsman Tybalt dearly,
And so did I. Well, we were born to die.
5   'Tis very late, she'll not come down tonight.
I promise you, but for your company,
I would have been a-bed an hour ago.

PARIS.   These times of woe afford no times to woo.
Madam, good night, commend me to your
        daughter.

10   LADY CAPULET.   I will, and know her mind early
        tomorrow;
Tonight she's mewed up to her heaviness.

PARIS *offers to go in, and* CAPULET *calls him again.*

CAPULET.   Sir Paris, I will make a desperate tender
Of my child's love. I think she will be rul'd
In all respects by me; nay more, I doubt it not.
15   Wife, go you to her ere you go to bed,
Acquaint her here of my son Paris' love,
And bid her—mark you me?—on We'n'sday next—
But soft, what day is this?

PARIS.   Monday, my lord.

CAPULET.   Monday! ha, ha! Well, We'n'sday is too
     soon,
20   A' Thursday let it be—a' Thursday, tell her,
She shall be married to this noble earl.
Will you be ready? do you like this haste?
We'll keep no great ado—a friend or two,
For hark you, Tybalt being slain so late,
25   It may be thought we held him carelessly,
Being our kinsman, if we revel much: .
Therefore we'll have some half a dozen friends,
And there an end. But what say you to Thursday?

PARIS.   My lord, I would that Thursday were
     tomorrow.

30   CAPULET.   Well, get you gone, a' Thursday be it
     then.—
[*To* LADY CAPULET] Go you to Juliet ere you go to bed,
Prepare her, wife, against this wedding-day.
Farewell, my lord. Light to my chamber ho!
Afore me, it is so very late that we
35   May call it early by and by. Good night.
                                        Exeunt.

FROM ACT III, SCENE V: **Capulet's orchard.**

LADY CAPULET.   . . . But now I'll tell thee joyful
     tidings, girl.

JULIET.   And joy comes well in such a needy time.
What are they, beseech your ladyship?

LADY CAPULET.   Well, well, thou hast a careful
     father, child,
5   One who, to put thee from thy heaviness,
Hath sorted out a sudden day of joy,

That thou expects not, nor I look'd not for.

JULIET.　Madam, in happy time, what day is that?

LADY CAPULET.　Marry, my child, early next Thursday morn,

10　The gallant, young, and noble gentleman,
The County Paris, at Saint Peter's Church,
Shall happily make thee there a joyful bride.

JULIET.　Now, by Saint Peter's Church and Peter too,

He shall not make me there a joyful bride.
15　I wonder at this haste, that I must wed
Ere he that should be husband comes to woo.
I pray you tell my lord and father, madam,
I will not marry yet, and when I do, I swear
It shall be Romeo, whom you know I hate,
20　Rather than Paris. These are news indeed!

LADY CAPULET.　Here comes your father, tell him so yourself;

And see how he will take it at your hands.

Enter CAPULET *and* NURSE.

CAPULET.　When the sun sets, the earth doth drizzle dew,

But for the sunset of my brother's son
25　It rains downright.
How now, a conduit, girl? What, still in tears?
Evermore show'ring? In one little body
Thou counterfeits a bark, a sea, a wind:
For still thy eyes, which I may call the sea,
30　Do ebb and flow with tears; the bark thy body is,
Sailing in this salt flood; the winds, thy sighs,
Who, raging with thy tears, and they with them,
Without a sudden calm, will overset
Thy tempest-tossed body. How now, wife?
35　Have you delivered to her our decree?

LADY CAPULET.　Ay, sir, but she will none, she gives you thanks.

I would the fool were married to her grave!

CAPULET.　Soft, take me with you, take me with you, wife.

How, will she none? Doth she not give us thanks?
40　Is she not proud? Doth she not count her blest,
Unworthy as she is, that we have wrought
So worthy a gentleman to be her bride?

JULIET.   Not proud you have, but thankful that you have.
Proud can I never be of what I hate,
45   But thankful even for hate that is meant love.

CAPULET.   How how, how how, chopp'd logic! What is this?
"Proud," and "I thank you," and "I thank you not,"
And yet "not proud," mistress minion you?
Thank me no thankings, nor proud me no prouds,
50   But fettle your fine joints 'gainst Thursday next,
To go with Paris to Saint Peter's Church,
Or I will drag thee on a hurdle thither.
Out, you green-sickness carrion! Out, you baggage!
You tallow-face!

LADY CAPULET.   Fie, fie, what, are you mad?

55   **JULIET.**   Good father, I beseech you on my knees,
Hear me with patience but to speak a word.

She kneels down.

CAPULET.   Hang thee, young baggage! disobedient wretch!
I tell thee what: get thee to church a' Thursday,
Or never after look me in the face.
60   Speak not, reply not, do not answer me!
My fingers itch. Wife, we scarce thought us blest
That God had lent us but this only child,
But now I see this one is one too much,
And that we have a curse in having her.
65   Out on her, hilding!

NURSE.   God in heaven bless her!
You are to blame, my lord, to rate her so.

CAPULET.   And why, my Lady Wisdom? Hold your tongue,
Good Prudence, smatter with your gossips, go.

NURSE.   I speak no treason.

CAPULET.   O, God-i-goden!

70   **NURSE.**   May not one speak?

CAPULET.   Peace, you mumbling fool!
Utter your gravity o'er a gossip's bowl,
For here we need it not.

LADY CAPULET.   You are too hot.

CAPULET.   God's bread, it makes me mad! Day, night, work, play,

Alone, in company, still my care hath been
75　To have her match'd; and having now provided
A gentleman of noble parentage,
Of fair demesnes, youthful and nobly lien'd,
Stuff'd, as they say, with honorable parts,
Proportion'd as one's thought would wish a man,
80　And then to have a wretched puling fool,
A whining mammet, in her fortune's tender,
To answer, "I'll not wed, I cannot love;
I am too young, I pray you pardon me."
But and you will not wed, I'll pardon you.
85　Graze where you will, you shall not house with me.
Look to't, think on't, I do not use to jest.
Thursday is near, lay hand on heart, advise.
And you be mine, I'll give you to my friend;
And you be not, hang, beg, starve, die in the streets,
90　For, by my soul, I'll ne'er acknowledge thee,
Nor what is mine shall never do thee good.
Trust to't, bethink you, I'll not be forsworn.

Exit.

JULIET.　Is there no pity sitting in the clouds,
That sees into the bottom of my grief?
95　O sweet my mother, cast me not away!
Delay this marriage for a month, a week,
Or if you do not, make the bridal bed
In that dim monument where Tybalt lies.

LADY CAPULET.　Talk not to me, for I'll not speak a
word.
100　Do as thou wilt, for I have done with thee.　*Exit.*

from *Characters of Shakespeare's Plays*
by William Hazlitt

William Hazlitt (1778–1830) was the son of a Unitarian minister whose outspoken support of the American and French revolutions led him to move his family from England to America when William was seven. The Hazlitts returned to England four years later, but William retained radical political convictions throughout his life. He studied painting but abandoned it and began his career as a writer in 1812. As a theater critic, Hazlitt examined the work of his contemporaries as well as the works of Shakespeare and other Elizabethan playwrights. His essays are renowned for their energy and enthusiasm; he preferred to state a topic and simply expand on it rather than structure his argument formally. Hazlitt described his own writing as "impressions" rather than criticism.

The Midsummer Night's Dream

Bottom the Weaver is a character that has not had justice done him. He is the most romantic of mechanics. And what a list of companions he has—Quince the Carpenter, Snug the Joiner, Flute the Bellows-mender, Snout the Tinker, Starveling the Tailor; and then again, what a group of fairy attendants, Puck, Peaseblossom, Cobweb, Moth, and Mustardseed! It has been observed that Shakespeare's characters are constructed upon deep physiological principles; and there is something in this play which looks very like it. Bottom the Weaver, who takes the lead of

> This crew of patches, rude mechanicals,
> That work for bread upon Athenian stalls,

follows a sedentary trade, and he is accordingly represented as conceited, serious, and fantastical. He is ready to undertake anything and everything, as if it was as much a matter of course as the motion of his loom and shuttle. He is for playing the tyrant, the lover, the lady, the lion. 'He will roar that it shall do any man's heart good to hear him'; and this being objected to as improper, he still has a resource in his good opinion of himself, and 'will roar you an 'twert any nightingale.' Snug the Joiner is the moral man of the piece, who proceeds by measurement and discretion in all things. You see him with his rule and compasses in his hand. 'Have you the lion's part written? Pray you, if it be, give it me, for I am slow of study.'—'You may do it extempore,' says Quince, 'for it is nothing but roaring.' Starveling the Tailor keeps the peace, and objects to the lion and the drawn sword. 'I believe we must leave the killing out when all's done.' Starveling, however, does not start the objections himself, but seconds them when made by others as if he had not spirit to express his fears without encouragement. It is too much to suppose all this intentional: but it very luckily falls out so. Nature includes all that is implied in the most subtle analytical distinctions; and the same distinctions will be found in Shakespeare. Bottom, who is not only chief actor, but stage-manager for the occasion, has a device to obviate the danger of frightening the ladies: 'Write me a prologue, and let the prologue seem to say, we will do no harm with our swords, and that Pyramus is not killed indeed; and for better assurance, tell them that I, Pyramus, am not Pyramus, but Bottom the Weaver; this will put them out of fear.' Bottom seems to have understood the subject of dramatic illusion at least as well as any modern essayist. If our holiday mechanic rules the roast among his fellows, he is no less at home in his new character of an ass, 'with amiable cheeks and fair large ears.' He instinctively acquires a most learned taste, and grows fastidious in the choice of dried peas and bottled hay. He is quite familiar with his new attendants, and assigns them their parts with all due gravity. 'Monsieur Cobweb, good Monsieur, get your weapon in your hand, and kill me a red-hipt humble-bee on the top of a thistle, and, good Monsieur, bring me the honey-bag.' What an exact knowledge is here shown of natural history!

Puck, or Robin Goodfellow, is the leader of the fairy band. He is the Ariel of the *Midsummer Night's Dream*; and yet as unlike as can be to the Ariel in *The Tempest*. No other poet could have made two such different characters out of the same fanciful materials and situations. Ariel is a minister of retribution, who is touched with a sense of pity at the woes he inflicts. Puck is a mad-cap sprite, full of wantonness and mischief, who laughs at those whom he misleads—'Lord, what fools these mortals be!' Ariel cleaves the air, and executes his mission with the zeal of a winged messenger; Puck is borne along on his fairy errand like the light and glittering gossamer before the breeze. He is, indeed, a most Epicurean little gentleman dealing in quaint devices and faring in dainty delights. Prospero and his world of spirits are a set of moralists: but with Oberon and his fairies we are launched at once into the empire of the butterflies. How beautifully is this race of beings contrasted with the men and women actors in the scene, by a single epithet which Titania gives to the latter, 'the human mortals'! It is astonishing that Shakespeare should be considered, not only by foreigners, but by many of our own critics, as a gloomy and heavy writer, who painted nothing but 'gorgons and hydras, and chimeras dire.' His subtlety exceeds that of all other dramatic writers, insomuch that a celebrated person of the present day said that he regarded him rather as a metaphysician than a poet. His delicacy and sportive gaiety are infinite. In the *Midsummer Night's Dream* alone, we should imagine, there is more sweetness and beauty of description than in the whole range of French poetry put together. What we mean is this, that we will produce out of that single play ten passages, to which we do not think any ten passages in the works of the French poets can be opposed, displaying equal fancy and imagery. Shall we mention the remonstrance of Helena to Hermia, or Titania's description of her fairy train, or her disputes with Oberon about the Indian boy, or Puck's account of himself and his employments, or the Fairy Queen's exhortation to the elves to pay due attendance upon her favorite, Bottom; or Hippolita's description of a chase, or Theseus's answer? The two last are as heroical and spirited as the others are full of luscious tenderness. The reading of this play is like wandering in a grove by moonlight: the descriptions breathe a sweetness like odors thrown from beds of flowers.

Titania's exhortation to the fairies to wait upon Bottom, which is remarkable for a certain cloying sweetness in the repetition of the rhymes, is as follows:

> Be kind and courteous to this gentleman.
> Hop in his walks, and gambol in his eyes,
> Feed him with apricocks and dewberries,
> With purple grapes, green figs and mulberries;
> The honey-bags steal from the humble bees,
> And for night tapers crop their waxen thighs,
> And light them at the fiery glow-worm's eyes,
> To have my love to bed, and to arise:
> And pluck the wings from painted butterflies,
> To fan the moon-beams from his sleeping eyes;
> Nod to him, elves, and do him courtesies.

The sounds of the lute and of the trumpet are not more distinct than the poetry of the foregoing passage, and of the conversation between Theseus and Hippolita:

> THESEUS. Go, one of you, find out the forester,
> For now our observation is perform'd;
> And since we have the vaward of the day
> My love shall hear the music of my hounds.
> Uncouple in the western valley, go,
> Dispatch, I say, and find the forester.
> We will, fair Queen, up to the mountain's top,
> And mark the musical confusion
> Of hounds and echo in conjunction.
>
> HIPPOLITA. I was with Hercules and Cadmus once,
> When in a wood of Crete they bay'd the bear
> With hounds of Sparta; never did I hear
> Such gallant chiding. For besides the groves,
> The skies, the fountains, every region near
> Seem'd all one mutual cry. I never heard
> So musical a discord, such sweet thunder.
>
> THESEUS. My hounds are bred out of the Spartan kind,
> So flew'd, so sanded, and their heads are hung

With ears that sweep away the morning dew;
Crook-knee'd and dew-lap'd, like Thessalian bulls,
Slow in pursuit, but matched in mouth like bells,
Each under each. A cry more tuneable
Was never halloo'd to, nor cheer'd with horn,
In Crete, in Sparta, nor in Thessaly:
Judge when you hear.

Even Titian never made a hunting-piece of a gusto so fresh and lusty, and so near the first ages of the world as this.

It had been suggested to us, that the *Midsummer Night's Dream* would do admirably to get up as a Christmas afterpiece; and our prompter proposed that Mr. Kean should play the part of Bottom, as worthy of his great talents. He might, in the discharge of his duty, offer to play the lady like any of our actresses that he pleased, the lover or the tyrant like any of our actors that he pleased, and the lion like 'the most fearful wild-fowl living.' The carpenter, the tailor, and joiner, it was thought, would hit the galleries. The young ladies in love would interest the side-boxes; and Robin Goodfellow and his companions excite a lively fellow feeling in the children from school. There would be two courts, an empire within an empire, the Athenian and the Fairy King and Queen, with their attendants and with all their finery. What an opportunity for processions, for the sound of trumpets and glittering of spears! What a fluttering of urchins' painted wings; what a delightful profusion of gauze clouds and airy spirits floating on them!

Alas, the experiment has been tried, and has failed; not through the fault of Mr. Kean, who did not play the part of Bottom, nor of Mr. Liston, who did, and who played it well, but from the nature of things. The *Midsummer Night's Dream*, when acted, is converted from a delightful fiction into a dull pantomime. All that is finest in the play is lost in the representation. The spectacle was grand; but the spirit was evaporated, the genius was fled.—Poetry and the stage do not agree well together. The attempt to reconcile them in this instance fails not only of effect, but of decorum. The ideal can have no place upon the stage, which is a picture without perspective: everything there is in the foreground. That which was merely an airy shape, a dream, a passing thought, immediately becomes an unmanageable reality. Where all is left to the imagination (as is the case in reading) every circumstance, near or remote, has an equal chance of being kept in mind, and tells according to the mixed impression of all that has been suggested. But the imagination cannot sufficiently qualify the actual impressions of the senses. Any offense given to the eye is not to be got rid of by explanation. Thus Bottom's head in the play is a fantastic illusion, produced by rnagic spells: on the stage, it is an ass's head, and nothing more; certainly a very strange costume for a gentleman to appear in. Fancy cannot be embodied any more than a simile can be painted; and it is as idle to attempt it as to personate Wall or Moonshine. Fairies are not incredible, but fairies six feet high are so. Monsters are not shocking, if they are seen at a proper distance. When ghosts appear at midday, when apparitions stalk along Cheapside, then may the *Midsummer Night's Dream* be represented without injury at Covent Garden or at Drury Lane. The boards of a theater and the regions of fancy are not the same thing.

Glossary

PRONUNCIATION KEY

VOWEL SOUNDS

a	hat	ō	go	ʉ	burn
ā	play	ô	paw, born	ə	extra
ä	star	o͡o	book, put		under
e	then	o͞o	blue, stew		civil
ē	me	oi	boy		honor
i	sit	ou	wow		bogus
ī	my	u	up		

CONSONANT SOUNDS

b	but	l	lip	t	sit
ch	watch	m	money	th	with
d	do	n	on	v	valley
f	fudge	ŋ	song, sink	w	work
g	go	p	pop	y	yell
h	hot	r	rod	z	pleasure
j	jump	s	see		
k	brick	sh	she		

a • bate (ə bāt´) *vt.,* make less in amount, degree, or force

a • bide (ə bīd´) *vi.,* submit to; put up with

a • mend (ə mend´) *vt.,* make better; improve

am • i • ty (am´i tē) *n.,* friendship

ap • pre • hen • sion (ap´rē hen´shən) *n.,* perception or understanding

apt (apt) *adj.,* suited to its purpose

a • sun • der (ə sun´dər) *adv.,* into parts or pieces

au • da • cious (ô dā´shəs) *adj.,* rudely bold

aus • ter • i • ty (ô ster´ə tē) *n.,* state of severe plainness and simplicity

bar • ren (bar´ən) *adj.,* sterile

be • guile (bē gīl´) *vt.,* deceive; charm; pass time pleasantly

be • queath (bē kwēth´) *vt.,* leave; pass on

be • seech (bē sēch´) *vt.,* ask for earnestly

bide (bīd) *vi.,* stay; continue; wait

bow • er (bou´ər) *n.,* place enclosed by overhanging boughs of trees

car • cass (kär´kəs) *n.*, human body, living or dead

chide (chīd) *vt.*, scold mildly

chron • i • cle (krän´ i kəl) *vt.*, tell or write the history of

clois • ter (klois´tər) *n.*, convent

con • cord (kän´ kôrd) *n.*, agreement; harmony

con • junc • tion (kən juŋk´shən) *n.*, a joining together; union

coun • ter • feit (kount´ ər fit´) *vt.*, make an imitation of to deceive

dale (dāl) *n.*, valley

dank (daŋk) *adj.*, disagreeably damp; moist and chilly

de • ri • sion (di rizh´ən) *n.*, contempt or ridicule

de • vise (di vīz´) *vt.*, contrive; plan

dis • cord (dis´ kôrd) *n.*, inharmonious combination of tones sounded together

dis • course (dis´ kôrs´) *vi.*, carry on conversation

dis • cre • tion (di skresh´ən) *n.*, power to act or judge; prudence

dis • par • age (di spar´ij) *vt.*, speak slightingly of

dis • patch (di spach´) *vt.*, send off or out promptly

dis • sem • ble (di sem´ bəl) *vt.*, conceal under a false appearance

dis • sen • sion (di sen´shen) *n.*, difference of opinion

dote (dōt) *vi.*, be excessively fond

dul • cet (dul´sit) *adj.*, soothing or pleasant to hear; sweet-sounding

e • dict (ē´dikt) *n.*, official public proclamation or order issued by authority; decree

en • am • or (en am´ər) *vt.*, fill with love and desire; charm; captivate

en • dure (en door´) *vt.*, bear, tolerate

en • mi • ty (en´mə tē) *n.*, hostility

en • sue (en soo´) *vi.*, come afterward; follow immediately

en • tice (en tīs´) *vt.*, attract by offering hope or reward of pleasure

en • treat (en trēt´) *vt.*, beg; beseech

es • teem (e stēm´) *vt.*, hold to be; consider; regard

ex • pound (eks pound´) *vt.*, explain or interpret

ex • tem • po • re (eks tem´pə rē) *adv.*, without preparation

filch (filch) *vt.*, steal

flout (flout) *vt.*, mock; show scorn or contempt for

for • sake (fôr sāk´) *vt.*, leave; abandon

for • swear (fôr swer´) *vt.*, renounce an oath; swear falsely

fray (frā) *n.*, noisy quarrel or fight

fren • zy (fren´ zē) *n.*, wild outburst of feeling or action

gait (gāt) *n.*, manner of moving on foot

gam • bol (gam´bəl) *vi.*, jump and skip about in play

gore (gôr) *n.*, blood shed from a wound

hab • i • ta • tion (hab´i tā´shən) *n.*, place in which to live

i • dol • a • try (ī däl´ə trē) *n.*, excessive devotion to a person or thing

im • brue (im brōō´) *vt.*, wet, soak, or stain, especially with blood

im • pair (im per´) *vt.*, make weaker

in • con • stant (in kän´stənt) *adj.*, fickle; unsteady in affections

in • suf • fi • cien • cy (in´sə fish´ən sē) *n.*, inadequacy

jol • li • ty (jäl´ə tē) *n.*, state of high spirits and good humor

keen (kēn) *adj.*, sharp or cutting

knav • ish (nāv´ish) *adj.*, dishonest; roguish; tricky

liv • er • y (liv´ər ē) *n.*, uniform

loath (lōth) *adj.*, unwilling; reluctant

mar (mär) *vt.*, injure or damage

masque (mask) *n.*, dramatic entertainment popular among the aristocracy of the sixteenth and seventeenth centuries, usually based on a mythical or allegorical theme and featuring lavish costumes, scenery, dancing, and music

mirth (murth) *n.*, joyfulness and merriment characterized by laughter

nup • tial (nup´shəl) *adj.*, of marriage or a wedding

o • di • ous (ō´dē əs) *adj.*, disgusting; offensive

of • fi • cious (ə fish´əs) *adj.*, offering unnecessary and unwanted advice; meddlesome

par • a • gon (par´ə gän´) *n.*, model or pattern of perfection or excellence

pert (purt) *adj.*, lively, jaunty

pre • pos • ter • ous • ly (prē päs´tər əs lē) *adv.*, absurdly; contrary to nature

prog • e • ny (präj´ə nē) *pl. n.*, descendants or offspring

prom • on • to • ry (präm´ən tôr´ē) *n.*, peak of high land that juts out into a body of water

pros • per • i • ty (prä sper´ə tē) *n.*, good fortune, wealth, and success

pro • verb (präv´ʉrb´) *n.*, short, traditional saying

rail (rāl) *vi.*, speak bitterly or reproachfully

rash (rash) *adj.*, too hasty in acting or speaking

re • buke (ri byo͞ok´) *vt.*, blame or scold in a sharp way

re • com • pense (rek´əm pens´) *n.*, something given to make up for a loss

re • count (ri kount´) *vt.*, tell in detail

rec • re • ant (rek´rē ənt) *n*, coward; traitor

sauc • y (sô´sē) *adj.*, impudent; pert

seeth • ing (sēth´iŋ) *adj.*, boiling; violently agitated

shun (shun) *vt.*, keep away from

sov • er • eign • ty (säv´rən tē) *n.*, the status or dominion of a ruler

span • gled (spaŋ´gəld) *adj.*, decorated with small bright objects that glitter

spurn (spʉrn) *vt.*, push or drive away contemptuously or scornfully

stat • ure (stach´ər) *n.*, height of a person

steep (stēp) *vt.*, immerse, saturate, absorb, or imbue

strife (strīf) *n.*, act or state of fighting or quarreling

sur • feit (sʉr´fit) *n.*, excess; too great an amount

swag • ger (swag´ər) *vi.*, boast, brag, or show off in a loud manner

tar • ry (tar´ē) *vi.*, stay for a time; remain temporarily

te • di • ous (tē´dē əs) *adj.*, long and tiresome

tes • ty (tes´tē) *adj.*, irritable; touchy

trans • fig • ure (trans fig´yər) *vt.*, transform

trip • ping • ly (trip´iŋ lē) *adv.*, lightly and quickly; nimbly

up • braid (up brād´) *vt.*, rebuke severely or bitterly

val • or (val´ər) *n.*, courage or bravery

ven • tur • ous (ven´chər əs) *adj.*, daring; inclined to take chances

vex • a • tion (veks ā´shən) *n.*, irritation, aggravation

vile (vīl) *adj.*, repulsive; disgusting

vis • age (viz´ij) *n.*, face

wag • gish (wag´ish) *adj.*, roguishly merry

wane (wān) *n.*, gradual decrease of the visible face of the moon after it has become full

war • ble (wôr´bəl) *vt.*, sing melodiously

wax (waks) *vi.*, increase in strength, intensity, volume (*waxen* is an archaic plural form of the verb; the modern form is *wax*)

wont • ed (wänt´id) *adj.*, customary; usual

woo (wo͞o) *vt.*, try to get the love of; seek as a spouse

Handbook of Literary Terms

Aim. A writer's **aim** is the primary purpose that his or her work is meant to achieve. One commonly used method of classifying writing by aim, proposed by James Kinneavey in *A Theory of Discourse,* describes four major aims: to express oneself (expressive writing), to persuade (persuasive writing), to inform (informative writing), and to create a work of literary art (literary writing).

Allusion. An **allusion** is a rhetorical technique in which reference is made to a person, event, object, or work from history or literature.

Character. A **character** is a person (or sometimes an animal) who figures in the action of a literary work. A *protagonist,* or *main character,* is the central figure in a literary work. An *antagonist* is a character who is pitted against a protagonist. *Major characters* play significant roles in a work. *Minor characters* play lesser roles. A *one-dimensional character, flat character,* or *caricature* is one who exhibits a single dominant quality, or *character trait.* A *three-dimensional, full,* or *rounded character* is one who exhibits the complexity of traits associated with actual human beings. A *static character* does not change during the course of the action. A *dynamic character* does change. A *stock character* is one found again and again in different literary works.

Climax. The **climax** is the point of highest interest and suspense in a literary work. The term also is sometimes used to describe the *turning point* of the action in a story or play, the point at which the rising action ends and the falling action begins. See *crisis* and *plot.*

Comedy. Originally a literary work with a happy ending, a **comedy** is any lighthearted or humorous work, especially one prepared for the stage or the screen. Comedy is often contrasted with tragedy, in which the hero meets an unhappy fate. (It is perhaps only a slight exaggeration to say that comedies end with wedding bells and tragedies with funeral bells.) Comedies typically present less-than-exalted characters who display all-too-human limitations, foibles, faults, and misunderstandings. The typical progression of the action in a comedy is from initial order to a humorous misunderstanding or confusion and back to order again. Stock elements of comedy include mistaken identity, word play, satire, and exaggerated characters and events.

Crisis. In the plot of a story or a drama, the **crisis** is that point in the development of the conflict at which a decisive event occurs that causes the main character's situation to become better or worse. See *plot*.

Dramatic irony. See *irony*.

Iamb. An **iamb** is a poetic foot containing one weakly stressed syllable followed by one strongly stressed syllable, as in the words *afraid* and *release*. A line of poetry made up of iambs is said to be *iambic*.

Inciting Incident. See *plot*.

Irony. Irony is a difference between appearance and reality. Types of irony include the following: *dramatic irony,* in which something is known by the reader or audience but unknown to the characters; *verbal irony,* in which a statement is made that implies its opposite; and *irony of situation,* in which an event occurs that violates the expectations of the characters, the reader, or the audience.

Mood. **Mood,** or **atmosphere,** is the emotion created in the reader by part or all of a literary work. A writer creates a mood through judicious use of concrete details.

Parody. A **parody** is a literary work that imitates another work for humorous, often satirical, purposes.

Plot. A **plot** is a series of events related to a central *conflict,* or struggle. A typical plot involves the introduction of a conflict, its development, and its eventual resolution. Terms used to describe elements of plot include the following:
- The **exposition,** or **introduction,** sets the tone or mood, introduces the characters and the setting, and provides necessary background information.
- The **inciting incident** is the event that introduces the central conflict.
- The **rising action,** or **complication,** develops the conflict to a high point of intensity.
- The **climax** is the high point of interest or suspense in the plot.
- The **crisis,** or **turning point,** often the same event as the climax, is the point in the plot where something decisive happens to determine the future course of events and the eventual working out of the conflict.
- The **falling action** is all of the events that follow the climax.
- The **resolution** is the point at which the central conflict is ended, or resolved.

- The **dénouement** is any material that follows the resolution and that ties up loose ends.
- The **catastrophe**, in tragedy, is the event that marks the ultimate tragic fall of the central character. Often this event is the character's death.

Plots rarely contain all these elements in precisely this order. Elements of exposition may be introduced at any time in the course of a work. A work may begin with a catastrophe and then use flashback to explain it. The exposition, dénouement, or even the resolution may be missing. The inciting incident may occur before the beginning of the action actually described in the work. These are but a few of the many possible variations that plots can exhibit.

Prose. **Prose** is the broad term used to describe all writing that is not drama or poetry, including fiction and nonfiction. Types of prose writing include novels, short stories, essays, and journalism. Most biographies, autobiographies, and letters are written in prose.

Pun. A **pun** is a play on words, one that wittily exploits a double meaning.

Satire. **Satire** is humorous writing or speech intended to point out errors, falsehoods, foibles, or failings. It is written for the purpose of reforming human behavior or human institutions.

Scene. A **scene** is a short section of a literary work that presents action that occurs in a single place or at a single time. Long divisions of dramas are often divided into scenes.

Setting. The **setting** of a literary work is the time and place in which it occurs, together with all the details used to create a sense of a particular time and place. Writers create setting by various means. In fiction, setting is most often revealed by description of such elements as landscape, scenery, buildings, furniture, clothing, the weather, and the season. It can also be revealed by how characters talk and behave. In its widest sense, setting includes the general social, political, moral, and psychological conditions in which characters find themselves.

Simile. A **simile** is a comparison using *like* or *as*.

Soliloquy. A **soliloquy** is a speech delivered by a lone character that reveals the speaker's thoughts and feelings.

Style. **Style** is the manner in which something is said or written. Traditionally, critics and scholars have referred to three levels of style: high style, for formal occasions or lofty subjects; middle style, for ordinary occasions or subjects; and low style, for extremely informal occasions or subjects. A writer's style depends upon many things, including his or her *diction* (the words that the writer chooses), selection of grammatical structures (simple versus complex sentences, for example), and preference for abstract or concrete words. Any recurring feature that distinguishes one writer's work from another's can be said to be part of that writer's style.

Suspension of Disbelief. Suspension of disbelief is the phrase used by poet and critic Samuel Taylor Coleridge in his *Biographia Literaria* to describe the act by which the reader willingly sets aside his or her skepticism in order to participate imaginatively in the work being read. The willingness to suspend disbelief, to participate imaginatively in a story being read, is the most important attribute, beyond literacy, that a person can bring to the act of reading.

Synaesthesia. Synaesthesia is a figure of speech that combines in a single expression images related to two or more different senses.

Verbal Irony. See *Irony.*